Nova Scotia's Historic Harbours

The Seaports that Shaped the Province

Joan Dawson

NIMBUS
PUBLISHING
NIMBUS.CA

Copyright © 2020, Joan Dawson

All rights reserved. No part of this book may be reproduced, stored in a retrieval system or transmitted in any form or by any means without the prior written permission from the publisher, or, in the case of photocopying or other reprographic copying, permission from Access Copyright, 1 Yonge Street, Suite 1900, Toronto, Ontario M5E 1E5.

Nimbus Publishing Limited
3660 Strawberry Hill Street, Halifax, NS, B3K 5A9
(902) 455-4286 nimbus.ca

Printed and bound in Canada

NB1461

Design: Jenn Embree
Editor: Elizabeth Eve

Library and Archives Canada Cataloguing in Publication

Title: Nova Scotia's historic harbours : the seaports that shaped the province / Joan Dawson.
   Names: Dawson, Joan, 1932- author.
   Description: Includes bibliographical references.
   Identifiers: Canadiana (print) 20200184997 | Canadiana (ebook) 20200185004 | ISBN 9781771088589 (softcover) | ISBN 9781771088596 (HTML)
   Subjects: LCSH: Harbors—Nova Scotia—History. | LCSH: Port cities—Nova Scotia—History. | LCSH: Nova Scotia—History.
Classification: LCC HE554.A3 D39 2020 | DDC 387.109716—dc23

Nimbus Publishing acknowledges the financial support for its publishing activities from the Government of Canada, the Canada Council for the Arts, and from the Province of Nova Scotia. We are pleased to work in partnership with the Province of Nova Scotia to develop and promote our creative industries for the benefit of all Nova Scotians.

 *To all those who came from away to Nova Scotia's harbours and made this place their home*

Table of Contents

Preface	1
Introduction	3
Bays and Harbours	6
Comings and Goings	8
The Fishery	12
Shipbuilding	16
Halifax's Harbours	19
"The Harbour of Chebucto"	19
Harbour Islands	27
Sambro and Devils Islands; McNabs, Lawlor, and Georges Islands	
Bedford Basin	32
The Northwest Arm	35
Melville and Deadmans Islands	
South Shore	39
St. Margarets Bay	39
Peggys Cove; Little Harbours on the Bay	
Mahone Bay	42
Chester; Town of Mahone Bay; The Tancooks; East Ironbound; Oak Island	
Lunenburg Bay and LaHave River	48
Lunenburg; LaHave River; LaHave, Riverport, and Bridgewater; LaHave Islands	

WESTWARD TO SHELBURNE	59
Liverpool Bay and Harbour; Coffin Island; Port Mouton; Shelburne Harbour; Birchtown; McNutts Island	
CAPE SABLE AREA	69
Port LaTour; Barrington Bay; Cape Sable Island; Shag Harbour	

ACADIAN SHORE — 76

PUBNICO HARBOUR	76
TOWNSHIP OF ARGYLE	79
Tusket; Wedgeport	
CHEBOGUE HARBOUR	82
YARMOUTH	83
ST. MARYS BAY	86
Cape St. Marys; Meteghan; Weymouth Harbour	

BAY OF FUNDY — 91

DIGBY NECK, LONG ISLAND, AND BRIER ISLAND	91
Sandy Cove	
ANNAPOLIS BASIN	95
The Port Royal Habitation; Port Royal and Annapolis Royal; Digby; Clementsport	
MINAS BASIN	102
Grand Pré, Horton, Mud Creek, and Port Williams; Avon River Estuary: Windsor, Hantsport, and Avondale; Cobequid Bay; Maitland and Truro	
CHIGNECTO SHORE	114
Parrsboro; Advocate Harbour	
CUMBERLAND BASIN	118
Beaubassin and Minudie	

NORTHUMBERLAND SHORE — 121

PUGWASH, WALLACE, AND TATAMAGOUCHE HARBOURS	121
PICTOU HARBOUR	124
ST. GEORGES BAY	130
Antigonish and Pomquet; Tracadie; Havre Boucher	

CAPE BRETON ISLAND	134
HARBOURS ON THE STRAIT OF CANSO	135
SYDNEY HARBOUR	135
GLACE BAY AND MORIEN BAY	139
Louisbourg	
ST. PETERS BAY	145
HARBOURS ON BRAS D'OR LAKE	147
Eskasoni; Big Harbour; Baddeck	
ST. ANNS HARBOUR	150
CHÉTICAMP	152
EASTERN SHORE	157
CHEDABUCTO BAY	157
Canso; Guysborough	
TOR BAY	162
COUNTRY HARBOUR AND ISAACS HARBOUR	164
ST. MARYS RIVER	166
LISCOMB HARBOUR	167
TANGIER HARBOUR	170
COLE HARBOUR, LAWRENCETOWN, AND CHEZZETCOOK	171
AFTERWORD	176
ACKNOWLEDGEMENTS	178
BIBLIOGRAPHY	179
IMAGE CREDITS	183

Preface

I'm what Maritimers call a CFA, or "come from away." I don't find the term offensive, merely a statement of fact. Except for Indigenous Peoples, all of us, or our ancestors sometime in the past, came from away. Over the years, people came to Nova Scotia for different reasons—some as explorers, fishers, or traders, some looking for work, some escaping from intolerable social or political conditions, some seeking adventure, or love, or a means to improve their status in society, some in the course of their military duties, and some quite accidentally. Whatever their motives, until well into the second half of the twentieth century, when air travel became more affordable and more convenient, most visitors and immigrants arrived in Nova Scotia through one of the province's many harbours.

I arrived in Halifax Harbour from England on a transatlantic steamship that carried passengers between Liverpool, St. John's, Halifax, and Boston. With a thirty-six-hour stopover in St. John's, the journey took ten days. This was a comfortable way to travel, and a stark contrast to what early settlers endured as their wooden sailing vessels lurched through the ocean for weeks, and even months, on their way from Europe. Food and water supplies often ran low, and without refrigeration, if the voyage was long, they were foul well before the vessel arrived. Travellers were packed into cramped spaces below decks, and in stormy weather, conditions must have been almost unendurable. Illness was common, some women gave birth in deplorable circumstances, and those people who died during the passage were buried at sea. Other settlers had a shorter voyage, on coastal vessels from elsewhere in the Maritimes or from ports on the Eastern Seaboard.

Whatever their origins, they were looking for new beginnings, and they came into Nova Scotia's harbours with hope in their hearts. Once they had disembarked, newcomers might face the daunting tasks of clearing land around the harbour, building homes, and somehow scraping a living from the lakes, the sea, and the forest.

Some of the communities they established were more successful than others, and all endured fluctuations in their economic lives. They witnessed battles, shipwrecks, privateering and piracy, celebrations, and tragedies. But Nova Scotia's coastal cities, towns, and villages began with the hard work of settlers who "came from away" and made this place their home.

I spend time in summer in a cottage overlooking a river where Mi'kmaw canoes once travelled, where some of the earliest French settlers landed, where ships were built in little coves, and where, in the nineteenth century, hundreds of merchant vessels came and went from the port at the head of tide. A harbour across the river was once home to a large fleet of fishing schooners, and inshore fishers worked from little harbours on the islands. Outfitters, fish packing plants, and ship owners operated in many small settlements. The sight and smell of the day's catch drying on fish flakes all along the shore was ever-present until the 1950s. All this has changed, but the rich history of our coastal communities is preserved in museums around the province, and in the work of local historians who ensure, in print or online, that the past is not forgotten. I am grateful to them.

—JD

Introduction

The beautiful harbours along Nova Scotia's rugged shoreline take many forms. Some are broad and studded with islands, others are long inlets carved out by glaciers during the last Ice Age. For thousands of years before Europeans came here, the rivers running into these waters brought the Indigenous Peoples from their inland winter communities to their summer fishing grounds around the harbours. The Mi'kmaq have lived for many centuries in what they call Mi'kma'ki, comprising the area that many of us now know as Nova Scotia. Traditionally, they had permanent and seasonal villages around the bays and coves, and along the shore. They had seasonal encounters with fishers from Europe for at least two centuries. The Mi'kmaq confirmed their alliance with the French through ceremonies, and later, ceremonial treaties were made with the British, followed by written treaties. The First Nations did not surrender their land, and though relations between them and the British were initially difficult, and remain imperfect, today we live together in peace and friendship.

European settlement began in the seventeenth century, and by the nineteenth century many harbours had been transformed into busy ports with shipyards, fishing vessels, fish processing plants, and merchant shipping. Today, Halifax Harbour is home to Nova Scotia's naval vessels, huge container ships, and massive cruise liners, and to smaller boats offering harbour tours, as well as ferries and private sailboats. Smaller, quieter harbours have wharves stacked with lobster traps, with fishing boats moored nearby.

Many of the sheltered harbours along the Atlantic coast were known to European fishing crews from about the time John Cabot was conducting his explorations in the late fifteenth century. In their wooden sailing vessels, they made the perilous journey across the Atlantic Ocean every spring and spent the summer fishing for cod. Most Europeans were then Roman Catholic, with obligatory fasting on Fridays and during the six weeks of Lent, during which time meat was forbidden although fish could be consumed. This resulted in a lucrative market for dried salt fish that could be stored and transported without spoilage for use when required. The fishing boats returned to Europe in the fall laden with processed fish, and also with another valuable commodity—furs.

After the spring melt the Mi'kmaq, who spent the winter inland, travelled to the coast. They harvested shellfish, as well as salmon and other inshore species. In this way, the people who had traditionally fashioned knives, tools, and weapons from stone first encountered the fishers whose implements were made of iron. A satisfying trading relationship was established when the Mi'kmaq brought furs which they exchanged for tools, implements, cloth, and decorative beads, all manufactured in France and Spain.

When Europeans came to colonize and establish settlements in eastern North America, the natural harbours were key to the development of viable communities. In the seventeenth century, France laid claim to the place they called Acadie, which encompassed much of present-day New Brunswick, Nova Scotia, and part of Maine. The earliest settlements consisted of fur-trading posts and fishing stations set up in sheltered harbours. Port Royal on the Annapolis Basin was the site of the first of these settlements. Here, as elsewhere, the newcomers were shown valuable survival skills by the Mi'kmaq and given the help that they needed to adapt to the environment, to survive the harsh winter, to find food, and to learn Indigenous cultural ways.

In the seventeenth and eighteenth centuries, when Britain and France were fighting for control of Nova Scotia, and at the time of the American Revolution, harbours were often scenes of conflict. Raiding parties attacked coastal communities, and shore-based defenders retaliated by storming enemy ships. But more peaceful times followed, and in the nineteenth century, many of Nova Scotia's harbours became busy trading ports, sending lumber, fish, and other exports to Europe and the Caribbean, as well as to even more distant places. Wooden sailing vessels were built in shipyards along the shore, close to a plentiful supply of wood. Fishing schooners set out to the offshore banks, and the inshore fishery flourished. The communities grew very quickly and new settlers built a prosperous society that helped make Nova Scotia what it is today.

The age of sail came to an end with the close of the nineteenth century, but fishing continued as a major occupation until the demise of the cod fishery in the second half of the twentieth century. Today, the catch is more diversified, and the lobster season is a much-publicized event. There are often more pleasure boats than fishing vessels at the wharves, and tourism—a major industry in Nova Scotia for almost a century—brings a great deal of activity to the coast during summer and fall.

Nova Scotia's harbours abound in legends of pirates and buried treasure. Although very few have any factual basis, the more credible tales are well worth retelling. In many instances, ships were seized and settlements raided by privateers—private operators who, unlike pirates, were authorized by their governments in times of war to attack shipping and destroy vessels, or take away cargo. Nova Scotians on shore were sometimes victims of these raids, and in their turn launched their own privateer vessels, bringing back ships, prisoners, and goods for which they received prize money.

Throughout history, human activities in this region have been mostly formed by proximity to the ocean, and most Mi'kmaw communities and major European settlements have developed around the bays and harbours. The shores of Nova Scotia have seen everything from seasonal fishing stations to modern fish packing plants, from informal trading posts to international commercial ports, from tiny fortified settlements to important military and naval bases, and from lumbering and shipbuilding villages to major industrial centres. In the following pages we shall follow coastal routes around the province, and see how its cities, towns and villages have been shaped by the sea. But first let us look at the diversity of these bays and harbours, and the activities that they supported.

Note on place names

I have generally used the French form of place names for periods of French occupation, and English forms after British settlement. Both French and English spellings sometimes vary over time. I have been guided by the forms used in The Canadian Geographical Names Database *where apostrophes are generally omitted. There are numerous French and English versions of Mi'kmaw place names, whose original forms are themselves variable, and their interpretations, when available, are often uncertain. Where possible, I have used forms found in* The Language of this Land, Mi'kma'ki, *by Trudy Sable and Bernie Francis.*

Bays and Harbours

―――♦―――

Nova Scotia's coastline consists in some areas of wide bays, that is, bodies of water that are indentations of sea into the land, defined by headlands and open to the ocean. The Bay of Fundy is the largest and longest, separating Nova Scotia from the mainland. The jagged coastline of the Eastern Shore and South Shore is cut by many long inlets and drowned river estuaries. Bays and coves offer shelter for vessels along the rocky Atlantic coast of Cape Breton Island, while the shallow inlets on the Gulf of St. Lawrence on the western side are havens for small boats.

The Bay of Fundy is notable for having the highest tides in the world as water from the Atlantic Ocean builds up as it flows into this long inlet. At its head, Cape Chignecto divides it into two smaller basins, forcing the water to rise even higher. At Burntcoat Head, on the Minas Basin, the tidal range can extend to over sixteen metres, the height of a five-storey building. The range on the Cumberland Basin is nearly as high. Everywhere on the Bay of Fundy, extensive mud flats can be found twice a day at low tide, leaving boats high and dry in its harbours, while by high tide they will be floating again. On the Atlantic coast and elsewhere, a much smaller tidal range allows vessels to use the harbours at any time.

So why have harbours always been so important in the history of Nova Scotia? From sheltered inlets, people can have access to the sea in safety. They can launch and tie up vessels on beaches and quays, confident that spurs of land, sandbars, curves in an estuary, and similar features, give protection from the powerful forces of wind and waves. This protection is often augmented by man-made seawalls.

The harbours visited in this book vary in size and depth, some able to accommodate large freighters while others are suitable for small fishing boats and pleasure craft. They are places of arrival and departure, of trade and commerce, and today, they attract tourists for their natural beauty and their historical significance.

Harbours in Nova Scotia have seen the arrival of immigrants, the departure of deportees and of disillusioned settlers. They have seen the comings and goings of villages, of industries, and of naval and military installations. They have witnessed events that have changed history.

Comings and Goings

Just as people today flock to the coast in summer, so, when the snow melted, the inhabitants of Mi'kma'ki travelled by canoe downstream to the estuaries to harvest seafood. For many, it was an annual community event, and they would trade with one another, exchange news, and enjoy celebrations. They lived off the land and the sea, so fishing and gathering of shellfish were important activities. As well as being regular meeting places for the Mi'kmaq, harbours are often sites with spiritual significance, where ceremonies were held, and where there are burial grounds, although these have not always been respected by the colonial authorities.

From the late sixteenth century, Basque, Spanish, Portuguese, and French fishers who came to harvest North Atlantic cod sheltered in harbours on the coast. Their arrival was greeted from the first with peace and friendship and they were given help by the Mi'kmaq, who allowed them to set up seasonal fishing stations. There they traded with one another, exchanging tools and other metal items for furs.

The fur trade brought the first French entrepreneurs who attempted to establish settlements in the early seventeenth century. They built fortified trading posts and supplied hat-makers at home with valuable beaver pelts, but circumstances forced many of them to sail away again. Those who eventually came and remained became known as Acadians. Their communities took root along the Fundy and the southwest coasts, never far from the harbours that were their link to the outside world. They were able to drain the marshes for farmland without impinging on Mi'kmaw hunting and fishing grounds.

For much of the eighteenth century, Britain and France were engaged in disputes over trade and territory in North America. This resulted in a situation that was politically unstable for the Acadians in their well-established communities.

The steamship Trusty *provided a passenger service on the LaHave River between Bridgewater and Riverport in the early twentieth century.*

War exacerbated tensions between the British governor and the Acadians. In addition, New England militia, who were British subjects, came north for periodic raids on the Acadian communities. The francophone settlers became pawns in this struggle for control of North America.

Serious British settlement began in 1749 with Cornwallis's arrival in Chebucto Harbour and the foundation of Halifax. It was consolidated by the arrival there in the early 1750s of ships carrying German, Swiss, and French Protestants. These immigrants were brought to counterbalance the Acadian Catholics, whom the British authorities feared as potentially supporting France. War between Britain and France exacerbated tensions between the British governor and the Acadians and resulted in the tragic events of 1755, when the governor ordered their deportation. Ships came to the harbours on the Cumberland and Minas Basins and English soldiers forced the residents onto them, often splitting up families, and sent them into exile. Five years later, groups of New Englanders, known as Planters, sailed into the same harbours to establish settlements. They took over many of the Acadian farms and their descendants became the fishers, lumber workers, shipbuilders, and traders of the nineteenth century.

Meanwhile, the Mi'kmaq found that British colonial forces were less respectful than the French, and initially resisted British intrusion into their territories, sometimes by force. Eventually treaties were established between the British and the Mi'kmaq guaranteeing certain rights—guarantees that were, unfortunately, not always honoured. Nevertheless, the Mi'kmaq shared their knowledge of the land and the coastline with settlers, making what seemed like a strange and hostile environment into a place they could call home.

The American Revolution (1765–1783) brought raiding privateers to the shores and, in retaliation, Nova Scotian vessels obtained letters of marque and set out in pursuit of enemy shipping. This led to some lively incidents in harbour waters, and to celebrations as successful captains sailed home with their prizes.

After the Revolution, the people who were loyal to the British Crown (Loyalists) arrived in Nova Scotian harbours, often as refugees, hoping to make a permanent settlement in the colony. Unfortunately many of them left within a few weeks, months, or years when they found that conditions were harsh. They were not prepared to clear the forest, build their own homes, and start to build businesses from scratch. Many came from the ruling elite in New England and the southern colonies. The newcomers included groups of Free Blacks who had earned their freedom by fighting for the British. When they had the opportunity, some of them took up an offer of land in Sierra Leone.

In the 1790s, a contingent of Maroons, who had escaped from slavery and taken refuge in the hills in Jamaica, were deported and brought into Halifax Harbour. They were employed in construction work on the Citadel and granted land. But they also did not settle happily, and in 1800, most of them also left for Sierra Leone.

Immigration to Nova Scotia grew during the nineteenth and twentieth centuries. The Highland Clearances and famine in Ireland brought many refugees to Nova Scotia in search of a better life. As industry developed in this period, shiploads of workers came from many countries, usually to Halifax or Sydney, to seek employment in mines and factories. Many of them boarded trains for other parts of Canada, where land was available and labour was needed. Today, their story is told in the Canadian Museum of Immigration at Pier 21, built on the site of an immigration shed where so many had first set foot in Nova Scotia.

Until the early twentieth century, British naval vessels were based for part of the year at Halifax's Dockyard. They were replaced by the Royal Canadian Navy, established in 1910. Activity in Halifax Harbour increased in wartime as it was an assembly point for transatlantic convoys in both world wars, and troops from across the country embarked from Halifax piers for overseas service. Many soldiers who returned from the Second World War had married British women. The men travelled home with their units, but their "war brides" arrived as immigrants at Pier 21 in Halifax, some with young children, and were helped on their way by officials and volunteers.

The commercial wharves and warehouses that lined the waterfronts of all the busy harbours, including Halifax and Sydney, have disappeared along with scheduled passenger liners. Immigrants now arrive by air, but the ports have been rebuilt to accommodate container ships and cruise ships, which bring hundreds of passengers to land for a few hours, and then leave again.

Before roads were constructed along the coast, all communication between harbour communities was by boat. Some merchants operated their own vessels, but during the nineteenth century entrepreneurs set up regular services linking neighbouring communities with each other and with Halifax. Often, even when there were roads, travel by sea was more comfortable and convenient than a bumpy coach journey.

Ferry services were established for travel to islands and to provide shortcuts across harbours and rivers, avoiding long journeys around the shore. Originally privately operated, most of them are now run by the provincial government. Ferries have crossed Halifax Harbour since 1752 and, until the Macdonald Bridge was opened just over two hundred years later, were the only practical way to travel between Halifax and Dartmouth. Today, the harbour ferries form part of the municipal transit service.

Fishermen still come and go in many of Nova Scotia's small harbours. Increasingly, private pleasure boats moor beside them at the wharves. Some bring travellers, but many are used by local people or summer residents for excursions in waters in and around our harbours. Summer visitors enjoy whale-watching trips, lobster suppers, and other attractions. These are interesting places with a variety of stories to tell, many of which begin with the seasonal journey of the Mi'kmaq who traditionally came every summer to gather clams, and which continue into the present day with its commercial fishery.

The Fishery

Fish formed an important component of the Indigenous Peoples' diets. They harvested their catch from the rivers and the shore, sometimes constructing stone weirs to force the fish to a point where smaller species like eel or gaspereau could be trapped in nets or woven baskets. Larger fish, such as sturgeon and salmon, were speared. In summer, families gathered at the river-mouths to harvest clams and other molluscs on the sandy beaches or mud flats from the Atlantic coast to the Bay of Fundy and the Northumberland Shore. When the catch was good, fish surplus to immediate requirements was smoked and dried for later use. Treaties have preserved the Mi'kmaw right to fish for a moderate livelihood at any season. This right was confirmed in 1999 by the Supreme Court of Canada after being challenged by non-Indigenous interests.

Many of the harbours where the Mi'kmaq traditionally lived were also known to early European fishers seeking safe havens as they began to exploit the cod that once was plentiful off these shores. By custom or agreement, certain fleets returned every year to the same harbours, as evidenced in place names like Spanish Bay and Portuguese Cove, which have endured over time. The fishers unloaded dories or other small boats to fish with lines, and settled down for a season's fishing, salting down their catches in the ships' holds. At the end of the summer they returned home with their bounty.

As colonization of North America began to take root in the seventeenth century, the fishery was controlled by the Company of New France, under the authority of the French king. The company granted fishing and trading rights to individuals, and poachers could have their vessels confiscated, as happened to Captain Rossignol in Liverpool Harbour in 1604. Later in the century, when disputes arose among rival companies and individuals, arbitration took place in France.

The French began to develop a land-based cod fishery, and fishing stations were established along the Atlantic coast in the mid-seventeenth century. Nicolas Denys, who created several of these stations, left a first-hand account, written towards the end of the century, of the process of catching and preserving the fish. Ships anchored in spring, and their captains and crews came ashore with supplies for processing the catch. They prepared the shore base where they would spend the summer, and built a structure, "like a hall covered with a ship's sail," in which the men would sleep in bunks. The fishing boats were prepared, staging was built where the catch was to be processed, and racks—flakes—were set up to dry the fish. The fish could also be dried on a stony beach.

Boats set out each morning for the fishing grounds, and the men fished with hooks and lines, each man having a line at each side of the boat. On their return, the cod was split and salted, and the processed fish washed and laid out on the flakes to dry. If the cod moved too far offshore, the fishers set up camps, known as *dégrats*, in coves along the coast with several days' supplies so they could process and salt the fish. At the end of the season, the ships, loaded with their catches, returned to their home ports.

This period saw the beginning of French settlement on the harbours. Nicolas Denys was among the first to establish year-round fishing communities with his settlements on Chedabucto Bay and St. Peters Harbour. Only a small proportion of those who had fished all summer remained over the winter, but land was cleared for farming and a mixed economy developed as more settlers were brought from France. The descendants of these early settlers became known as Acadians.

When New Englanders settled in Nova Scotia in the second half of the eighteenth century, the population along the Atlantic coast increased and schooners set out for the fishing grounds in greater numbers. New England whalers also came and set up processing plants in Dartmouth and other places.

The American Revolution led to disputes over the fishery off Nova Scotia. Agreements about American access to Canadian waters between Nova Scotia and, after Confederation (1867), between Canada and the United States, were made and cancelled several times before the end of the nineteenth century.

In the 1800s, fishing boats left from every little harbour. Ports like Lunenburg had important schooner fleets fishing for cod on the Grand Banks off Newfoundland. Merchants outfitted ships, bought and processed the catch, exported it, and brought in goods for sale at their company stores. Some large fishing companies, such as the Robin brothers from the Isle of Jersey in the Channel Islands, who operated in Cape Breton, made enormous profits at the expense of the fishers who were paid only with credit at the company stores.

Cod remained the backbone of the Nova Scotia fishery well into the twentieth century. Processing methods remained much the same as in Denys's day. As late as the 1950s, fish flakes lined the harbour shores. The cod fishery was primarily an export industry, but the expansion of settlement in the eighteenth and nineteenth centuries saw an increased domestic market for other species such as haddock, herring, and mackerel, caught by inshore fishers. Trout and salmon were harvested from the rivers and estuaries, while clams, oysters, and other shellfish were gathered along the shores. For some species, like herring and mackerel, weirs were used, with nets supported on poles in which fish were trapped. This time-honoured method has continued in different parts of the Bay of Fundy into modern times, with circular nets on poles into which fish swim at high tide; they can then easily be harvested when the tide recedes.

While the cod fishery continued to rely on salting and drying for processing the catch, in the nineteenth century, canneries were established throughout Nova Scotia, from Chéticamp to Clarks Harbour, to process lobster for export. Lobster, once considered a poor man's food, had become a popular luxury item. Other methods of preservation were smoking, chiefly used for herring and haddock, and pickling, popular for herring.

The early twentieth century saw the introduction of trawlers by large companies, resulting in a much larger catch and a slump in prices that hurt the fishery. A bonanza for many was the introduction of Prohibition in the US in the 1920s, when money was to be made by rum-running—that is, smuggling alcohol into US ports. Hard times came again during the Great Depression in the 1930s, until the Second World War stimulated the economy.

Meanwhile, the government brought in stricter regulations to control and protect the fishery. The increased use of refrigerated fishing vessels in the second half of the century had a dual impact on the cod fishery. It replaced other methods to a great extent and allowed fish to be brought ashore in good condition. In Nova Scotia, large companies operated trawler fleets and established processing plants in places like Lunenburg and Canso. But new technology also brought foreign factory-freezer trawlers to the offshore fishing grounds, where they netted huge quantities of cod, discarded the bycatch (fish other than cod), and destroyed the habitats of other species.

In 1977, Canada's fishing limits were extended to two hundred nautical miles from the coast, excluding the foreign fleets that were depleting the groundfish stocks. With the dramatic decline of these stocks, actions were taken to regulate the fishery. In 1979, the federal government established the Department of Fisheries and Oceans (DFO), issuing licenses, establishing quotas, and controlling zones in which fishing is limited to certain times of the year. By 1992, the cod stocks had declined to such an extent that DFO stepped in and declared a moratorium on cod fishing. At the same time fishers were encouraged to bring in different species of fish.

Today, government control of the fishery offers encouragement to the industry while maintaining measures to prevent overfishing. There has been some controversy over DFO's Small Craft Harbours program, which has been beneficial in providing resources to some communities while others still wait for assistance. Also, some lobster fishers who have entered into controlling agreements with large companies may be forced to surrender their licences, which are meant to protect independent operators. The right of the Mi'kmaq to fish at all seasons to make a moderate living has been challenged, and upheld.

The fishery is a vital part of the Nova Scotia economy, and fish stocks are closely monitored. The cod stocks have not recovered as expected, and the moratorium is still in place, but after some years of depression in the industry, the fishery today is reviving with a greater diversification of the catch. The time of the lucrative lobster season varies in different areas and "Dumping Day"—when the first traps are set—is an important event in fishing communities. There is a good market for crab, shrimp, scallops, and other shellfish. The wild salmon stock, which was depleted by pollution, remains low, but fish farms around the coast have been established with varying degrees of success, and they remain controversial for several reasons, including their environmental impact and aspects of animal husbandry.

Fishing has always been a dangerous business: many lives have been lost over the years. Even with today's technology, fishing crews must still contend with wind, waves, and frigid temperatures in order to make a living from the sea. Modern vessels have become more capable of withstanding storms, and improved weather forecasting warns fishers of potentially hazardous conditions. Fishing boats are now equipped with radios and electronic devices, and safety regulations have been brought in to increase their security. Enormous changes have taken place since the days of wooden schooners, and now the most up-to-date technology protects the lives of ships' crews.

Shipbuilding

Over the years, shipbuilders in Nova Scotia have constructed all kinds of craft from birchbark canoes to wooden vessels, fibreglass-hulled Cape Islanders, and ships for the Canadian Navy.

When Europeans first came here, they observed the Mi'kmaq paddling canoes made of cedar frames covered with birchbark and caulked with pitch from spruce gum or pine resin. The canoes were light, and small ones could be carried by one person over portage trails between the lakes and rivers that were their highways. Other canoes were large, with high sides; they could carry freight, and were strong enough for use on the ocean. The Indigenous Peoples were skilled boat builders, and there are Mi'kmaw artisans today who construct birchbark canoes.

The early settlers came in square-rigged ships from France, but they brought carpenters who could replicate the smaller vessels, known as *chaloupes* or shallops, that were carried aboard the larger ships. These were open single-masted sailboats used for fishing and local travel. The first record we have of shipbuilding in Nova Scotia is from 1606 when François Gravé Dupont built a barque and a shallop at Port Royal.

Once settlements were established later in the century, carpenters were among the tradesmen recruited to join them, but the Acadians did not become large-scale shipbuilders, and it was left to others to establish what was to become a major Nova Scotian industry: the manufacture of wooden sailing vessels.

In 1760, New Englanders began to come to Nova Scotia at the governor's invitation to rebuild the rural economy after the Expulsion of the Acadians. Among those who came to the so-called "Planter" townships on the Atlantic coast were fishers and merchants who needed vessels, as well as men with skills to build them. Diarist Simeon Perkins, who established one of Liverpool's first sawmills, records that he had two schooners built in 1765.

Detailed records of shipbuilding at this time are scanty, but the industry grew quickly as the population expanded. Logs were floated down rivers like the Mersey to water-powered sawmills, which supplied the shipbuilders with lumber. By the end of the eighteenth century, Nova Scotia was producing vessels to carry away increasing quantities of fish and lumber, and to bring in goods from overseas.

The colony's flourishing economy in the nineteenth century was based on the export of fish, lumber, and agricultural produce. Its vast forest resources could supply the international market with lumber, and sawmills supplied both the export market and the needs of local shipyards. Shipwrights, sailmakers, blacksmiths, rope-makers, and other skilled craftspeople all contributed to the construction of a ship. At the height of the age of sail, in the second half of the nineteenth century, shipyards could be found in a great many Nova Scotian harbours, both large and small. They built vessels for local fishermen and merchants, as well as for clients in other parts of the world.

The vessels used for fishing were chiefly schooners, and many were built in the harbours from which they would operate. They usually had two or three masts, with diagonal spars supporting sails set along the line of the keel. This was known as the fore-and-aft or schooner rig. Schooners could move at high speed and required only a small crew, giving maximum space in the hold for fish or merchandise. Fishing schooners carried dories—small open boats that were built in dory shops or small boatyards.

Schooners were also used for trade, but many of the merchant vessels built in Nova Scotia were square-rigged vessels, with a series of horizontal spars supporting the sails. These included brigs with two masts, barques with three or more masts, and brigantines and barquentines, with two and three masts respectively and combinations of square-rigged and fore-and-aft sails. The largest ships had three or more masts, all square-rigged.

An interesting sidelight to the shipbuilding industry in the nineteenth century was its influence on Nova Scotia's building styles. The homes, churches, public and commercial buildings of this time were built in wood by carpenters who also worked in the shipyards and applied their methods to these structures. Their heavy beams were often supported by the same brackets—ships' knees—that supported the decks of ships. These were made from the bases of trees where there is a natural right angle in the grain from the trunk to the root, forming a strong support. It is no coincidence that the roofs of some churches look rather like upturned boats.

The age of sail brought prosperity to coastal communities, which resulted in population growth and a demand for the houses and public buildings that line the streets of today's towns and rural communities. But in other parts of the world, shipyards were launching iron-hulled steamships, and by the turn of the century, international shipping relied more on steam than on sail. Fishing methods were also changing, and although schooners continued to sail to the Grand Banks and Labrador in the first decades of the twentieth century, iron-hulled trawlers began to appear in Nova Scotia's harbours, and shipbuilders fell on hard times. Most small shipyards lacked the resources or skills to build in iron, and they were forced to close. Those that survived saw a decline in their business, with repair and maintenance of existing vessels providing more work than building new ones. Shipwrights, sailmakers, and other tradespeople were forced to move away to seek work and the population in the shipbuilding communities shrank.

Construction was revived in some shipyards in the 1920s, when rum-runners were taking advantage of Prohibition in the United States and Canada to make large profits by smuggling liquor. Local shipyards built low-profile, high-speed vessels known as banana boats, designed to elude the American customs officers who patrolled the coasts. This all came to an end in 1933 when the ban on producing and selling alcohol was lifted.

Shipyards received another boost in the Second World War with the urgent need for vessels. Yards at Pictou constructed freighters to transport supplies to Britain, while the Halifax Shipyard built destroyers for the Royal Canadian Navy and was a centre for repair and maintenance. This was the beginning of the construction of naval vessels in Halifax that continues today.

Boatyards can still be found in some other harbour communities, although large vessels are no longer built. Innovations in the fishing industry took place in the early twentieth century. The first was the design of the Cape Island boat, thought to have been invented in 1905 in Clarks Harbour on Cape Sable Island. This style of boat, with some practical modifications, is still built today and is used by many Maritime fishers because of its stability. The second was the invention of the two-cylinder make-and-break gasoline engine, in about 1910. This simple engine could be fitted to fishing boats that had previously been rowed or that relied on sails for propulsion. Also in the early twentieth century, some fishing schooners were equipped with auxiliary engines so they were not dependent solely on wind power.

With the recent diversification of the fishing industry, construction of specialized craft has increased. Many boatyards produce more pleasure boats than working vessels and undertake more maintenance than new construction. Fibreglass has replaced wood and most sails are made of synthetics rather than canvas, but Nova Scotia's boat builders are still respected for their skill and enterprise.

Halifax's Harbours

The deep estuary on Nova Scotia's Atlantic coast generally known as Halifax Harbour is home to the province's most active port. Sambro Island lies to the west of the wide entrance, and Devils Island to the east. McNabs, Lawlor, and Georges Islands protect the main harbour, which narrows at the north between Halifax and Dartmouth, then opens to another wide expanse of water, the Bedford Basin, into which the Sackville River flows. The long inlet known as the Northwest Arm forms the peninsula on which the city stands. Halifax Harbour, the Bedford Basin, and the Northwest Arm are three distinct bodies of water, each with its own story.

"THE HARBOUR OF CHEBUCTO"

Visitors coming into Halifax Harbour on a cruise ship today see tall buildings lining both shores, two bridges spanning the Narrows, ferries criss-crossing the shipping lane, and in the distance, naval vessels lying at their moorings. There are always container ships in port, and private craft of all kinds are travelling the length of this mighty harbour.

A very different scene greeted Edward Cornwallis when he sailed into what the map-makers called "The Harbour of Chebucto" with his settlers in 1749 to establish the new capital of Nova Scotia. Forests came down to the water on all shores, and the only other vessels were the canoes of the inhabitants of the area—the Mi'kmaq—who called this place K'jipuktuk, the Big Harbour. For thousands of years they had lived around its shores, hunted in the nearby forest, and fished in its waters. For them, an area near the tip of the peninsula, from what is now downtown Halifax to Point Pleasant Park, was a place of spiritual significance. Every spring, Mi'kmaw families travelled long distances to conduct ceremonies at the area called Amntu'kati, the place of spirits, celebrating the creation of their people.

It is likely, but unrecorded, that Europeans had sheltered their vessels in the harbour for many years prior to Cornwallis's fleet's arrival. Champlain had passed by briefly on his return journey to France in 1607 and described the harbour as very *saine*—meaning "healthful." In 1680 a French fishing company established a small base, but it was short-lived. By the end of the decade, only one Acadian family was living there among the Mi'kmaq. A French traveller, Marin Dièreville, passing through here in 1699, noted the abandoned fishing station. Dièreville described an encounter with two Mi'kmaq, armed with hatchets and rifles. On learning that the newcomers were French, the warriors made them welcome.

The occasional presence of French fishing boats had made very little impact on the Mi'kmaq of K'jipuktuk, but the arrival in 1746 of the remnants of a French fleet led by the duc d'Anville, devastated by sickness, proved disastrous. The diseases that were brought by the sailors and passengers on the ships spread among the Mi'kmaq in the area and beyond, and caused many deaths.

After this experience, the arrival of British settlers three years later was understandably unwelcome. In the spring of 1749, Edward Cornwallis sailed into the Harbour of Chebucto with a fleet of fourteen ships, led by the *Sphinx*, bringing about 2,500 British settlers and supplies with which to establish a garrison town on the west side of the harbour. He named it Halifax, after the British official in charge of colonies, George Montagu Dunk, Second Earl of Halifax.

Cornwallis's selection of Amntu'kati for the establishment of his settlement was particularly unfortunate. He ignored Mi'kmaw requests to find another site, and this insensitive action set the stage for the years of hostility that followed, with loss of life on both sides.

The newcomers were mostly poor Londoners, who lived on the ships or in tents on Georges Island until they had built their simple log houses. Land was cleared and surveyors laid out a grid pattern of streets on the steep hillside, with a parade square at its centre. Construction proceeded slowly because the settlers were largely unskilled. A sawmill was set up across the harbour where wood was cut for frame houses for the governor and the better-off colonists. When the *Alderney* arrived in 1750 with more colonists, they settled on the east side of the harbour, laying the foundations for the town of Dartmouth.

The early days of settlement were not easy. The Mi'kmaq understandably resented the establishment of Halifax, and of the secondary settlement across the harbour, because the land was being carved off into plots and their own settlements, paths, and hunting areas were made inaccessible. While attacking the sawmill in Dartmouth, they killed some workers. The British were brutal in their retaliation

The Town and Harbour of Halifax... by Richard Short depicts Halifax in 1764, with shipping in the harbour and some military defences on Georges Island.

for this event, sparking further confrontations and resentment among the Mi'kmaq that still simmers today.

Halifax's original fortifications consisted of a picket fence and several small forts, of which the largest would become the site of the Halifax Citadel. Other defences were built around the harbour in the following years. Georges Island was fortified, and several gun batteries were installed at Point Pleasant, between the main harbour and the Northwest Arm, guarding the entrance to both. In today's Point Pleasant Park, the Prince of Wales Tower, built in 1796, was the first of a series of round towers built in the late eighteenth and early nineteenth centuries to defend the harbour. A second, the Duke of York's Tower, now known as York Redoubt, overlooked the entrance, and a third, Fort Clarence, was built on the Dartmouth side. Fort Ogilvie was constructed at Point Pleasant during the Napoleonic Wars, and the defences there were upgraded and reused from time to time up until the end of the Second World War. Submarine nets were extended across the harbour mouth during both world wars.

In May 1751, four shiploads of European emigrants left Rotterdam, and in July the first vessel, the *Speedwell*, sailed into Chebucto Harbour. She was followed by the *Gale*, the *Pearl*, and the *Murdoch*, and altogether nearly one thousand Protestant settlers from Germany, France, and Switzerland disembarked in Halifax. The following year, they were joined by more "Foreign Protestants." Most of them sailed out again in 1753 to resettle in Lunenburg.

The Halifax waterfront was originally a beach sloping down to the water, and a gallows and stocks stood prominently by the shore, with the double purpose of punishment and deterrent. This was not the only site for punishment. In 1785, two pirates were hanged on Georges Island, and in 1809, a pirate by the name of Jordan was hanged near Black Rock Beach, at what is now Point Pleasant Park. No doubt this event attracted a good crowd of spectators.

Before wharves were constructed, transport and supply ships moored out in the channel, and passengers and freight were carried ashore in small boats. When enterprising New Englanders came to Halifax, merchants began to build wharves and warehouses along the shore.

Halifax Harbour has always been a strategic port in wartime. In 1757 and 1758, the British Navy was preparing its final assault on Louisbourg. The ships assembled in Halifax Harbour included HMS *Pembroke*, whose master was James Cook, later known for his explorations in the Pacific. Here, Cook met Samuel Holland, an experienced military surveyor, from whom he learned the art of charting coastal waters. After the fall of Louisbourg, Cook took part in the siege of Quebec, where his surveying skills enabled the British fleet to reach its destination. He then returned to Halifax, making charts of the town and the harbour before sailing for England in 1762.

These early years helped ensure that Halifax became a major military and naval base, as well as the administrative and commercial centre of the province. The first Citadel and barracks and the Naval Dockyard were begun in the late 1750s and were altered and expanded over the years. Prince Edward, Duke of Kent, who was the military commander in the late seventeenth century, set up a visual telegraph system allowing communication from York Redoubt to the forts in the harbour and to the Citadel. This device was used to announce approaching vessels, and for many years was put to both military and commercial use.

The Naval Dockyard on the western side of the harbour became one of the two North Atlantic stations for the Royal Navy, where crews were mustered, and vessels were maintained and repaired before setting out to sea. In the days of wooden ships, damaged masts and sails had to be replaced, and vessels careened to clear debris from their hulls. A tall sheerlegs (a kind of crane) stood on the edge of the

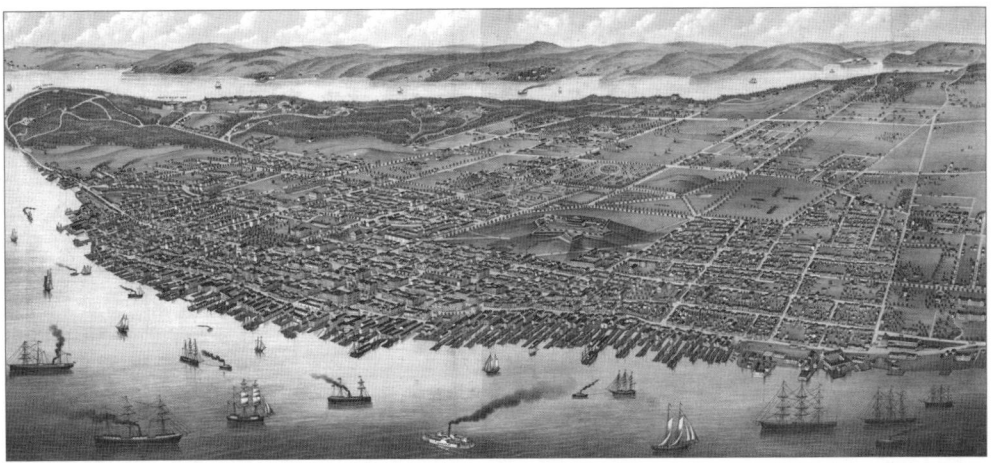

This bird's-eye view of Halifax in 1879 shows the busy commercial wharves and warehouses along the waterfront. Some steam-powered vessels are among the sailing ships in the harbour.

harbour for installing masts on the warships. A fine stone house was built for the Admiral that is still standing and serves as a naval museum.

The American Revolution (1765–1783) and later, the War of 1812, brought American privateers to Nova Scotia's shores, and vessels of the Royal Navy set out from the Dockyard to defend British interests. Bystanders near the waterfront witnessed a triumphant moment in 1813 when the British frigate HMS *Shannon* sailed into harbour with the USS *Chesapeake* and her crew, captured in Boston Harbor. British naval vessels used Halifax as a base during the Napoleonic wars, and continued to do so until the early twentieth century when the newly minted Naval Force of Canada, later to become the Canadian Navy, equipped with the second-hand British cruiser *Niobe*, took over the Dockyard.

In the nineteenth century, the waterfront was lined with merchants' wharves and warehouses, and there was constant traffic as trading vessels sailed in and out of what became a busy commercial port. The ice-free harbour allowed shipping to continue year-round, but in practice winter was a slack time because of Atlantic storms, so the arrival of ships from Britain, in spring, was a particular occasion for excitement. Their sighting brought citizens to the waterfront eagerly awaiting news of their relatives, their business interests, or the latest political events.

Industries grew up in both Halifax and Dartmouth, where the receiving of raw materials and the export of finished goods brought prosperity and growth to the region. One of the best-known entrepreneurs from Halifax was Samuel Cunard

George D. Troop's wharf in Dartmouth Cove, 1885. Merchant vessels like this carried goods in and out of the cove.

who ran a profitable import and export business for which he acquired a fleet of wooden vessels, later replaced by steamships. He was awarded the first contract for transatlantic mail, and his fleet developed into the well-known Cunard passenger line. During the nineteenth century Dartmouth was home to a variety of industries, and merchant vessels brought in raw materials and carried away finished goods. Dartmouth Cove was at one time the southern terminus of the Shubenacadie Canal, linking Halifax Harbour with the Shubenacadie River and the Minas Basin, following the traditional Mi'kmaw route across Nova Scotia. Canal construction began in 1826 and after many setbacks was finally completed in 1861. For a few years, boats and barges carried heavy goods, like lumber and minerals, along the canal. The steep ascent from the canal basin at Dartmouth Cove was achieved by means of an inclined hydraulic plane, a feat of engineering that lifted boats from the harbour to the upper level. The coming of the railway made the canal obsolete for carrying freight, and it ceased operation in 1871.

After the sinking of the *Titanic* in April 1912, ships from Halifax went to help with recovery and returned with the bodies of many of the drowned passengers. The ships and crew were met by hearses which conveyed the bodies to a temporary morgue, and the victims were buried in Halifax cemeteries.

Before industrial activity took over the waterfronts in Halifax and Dartmouth, there were many fishing vessels coming and going and, for a time, Dartmouth was home to Quaker whalers from New England, who processed their catch there. The Quaker House Museum in downtown Dartmouth tells their story.

Until late in the twentieth century, it was possible to buy fish directly from a company operating on the Halifax waterfront. Herring Cove, Portuguese Cove, and other small inlets on the outer harbour once sheltered dozens of fishing boats. Today, fishing boats have mostly vanished from the inner harbour, except for occasional visits by herring seiners. Nevertheless, fishing boats still frequent the picturesque Fisherman's Cove Heritage Centre, a restored fishing village at Eastern Passage.

Halifax saw a vast increase in military and naval personnel during the First World War. Traffic was busy in the harbour as ships passed in and out of Bedford Basin, where convoys were assembled to carry much-needed supplies overseas. On December 6, 1917, an accident of unprecedented proportions took place in the Narrows which separate the main harbour from Bedford Basin. A French ship, *Mont Blanc*, loaded with munitions, collided with Norwegian freighter *Imo*, and caught fire. The first vessel of the Canadian Navy, *Niobe*, sent men to try to assist, but the quantity of explosives on the *Mont Blanc* resulted in the largest man-made explosion before the atomic bomb. It killed many of the crew and destroyed a huge area of the north end of Halifax and much of Dartmouth. About two thousand people were killed, many more injured, and thousands made homeless. The disaster left many people scarred, blinded, and traumatized, and reconstruction took some time. One hundred years later, this tragedy is memorialized annually on December 6, particularly at the Memorial Bell Tower at Fort Needham.

As the twentieth century progressed, the port had to adapt to major changes in shipping and transportation. These changes accelerated with the outbreak of the Second World War, which brought an increased military and naval presence to the harbour. In addition to the convoys that assembled in Bedford Basin, there were many people coming to the port to aid the war effort, and soldiers embarking on troop ships for overseas service. Thousands of war brides coming to Canada passed through the immigration sheds at Pier 21, many with babies or small children.

The growth of airline services after the Second World War brought changes to the harbour. Fewer merchant ships used the wharves along the waterfront, commercial activities decreased, and passenger service declined. The Imperial Oil refinery, established in 1918 on the site of Fort Clarence on the Dartmouth shore, brought large tankers into the harbour. Its flares lit up the night sky until it was closed in 2013. Then, mid-century, containerization transformed the shipping industry.

A major addition was the Autoport in Eastern Passage, where incoming vehicles from distant places are transferred from freighters to car carriers for distribution by rail to their destinations. On the Halifax side, as the wharves and warehouses were taken down because they were no longer in use, a few of the oldest commercial buildings, known as the Historic Properties, were preserved and renovated to house shops, restaurants, and offices. A casino and several hotels were developed in the same area to attract visitors to the city, and there are now many modern residential condominium buildings on the waterfront, as well as restaurants and shops.

Continuing south, we come to the commercial wharves at Halifax Seaport and the Canadian Museum of Immigration at Pier 21, where the cruise ships discharge their passengers. Finally, just before Point Pleasant Park, there is the Halterm container terminal where freight is transferred to trains or trucks.

North from the downtown is the Canadian Navy Dockyard and the Irving Shipbuilding facilities where vessels are built and repaired.

From early days, a ferry has been a constant link between Halifax and Dartmouth, powered initially by oars and sails, and later by horses, steam, and finally today, by diesel engines. Two late nineteenth-century attempts to bridge the harbour failed, following the predictions of a curse said to have been laid on the water by a Mi'kmaw chief many years ago after his son's drowning. Presently there are two road bridges spanning the Narrows, opened in 1955 and 1970.

Over the years, the harbour has welcomed many distinguished visitors. In January 1842, Charles Dickens and his wife arrived in the harbour to begin their tour of North America. It was not an auspicious beginning: their ship, *Britannia*, ran aground off Eastern Passage and they had to wait for the rising tide. Things seemed better the following morning. Dickens wrote:

> Now, we were gliding down a smooth, broad stream, at the rate of eleven miles an hour: our colours flying gaily; our crew rigged out in their smartest clothes; our officers in uniform again; the sun shining as on a brilliant April day in England; the land stretched out on either side, streaked with light patches of snow; white wooden houses; people at their doors; telegraphs working; flags hoisted; wharfs appearing; ships; quays crowded with people; distant noises; shouts; men and boys running down steep places towards the pier: all more bright and gay and fresh to our unused eyes than words can paint them.

Among the less fortunate passengers to Halifax was Adèle Hugo, the daughter of the famous French writer Victor Hugo, who arrived in 1863 on board the New York mail packet. She was in pursuit of a certain Lieutenant Pinson, who had been posted to Nova Scotia with his regiment. She lived in Halifax, becoming increasingly mentally unstable, obsessed with her love for Pinson, until 1866, when once again she followed the gentleman to his next posting.

Halifax Harbour has welcomed and bidden farewell to many members of the royal family over the years. Prince Edward, the fourth son of George III, arrived in May 1794 to take command of British forces in the Maritimes. The ship bearing his mistress, Julie de St-Laurent, came into the harbour three months later. Since then, Halifax Harbour has welcomed many other royals, including King George VI and Queen Elizabeth II, Prince Philip, and Prince Charles.

The "Big Harbour" has seen many changes. Both the Halifax and Dartmouth waterfronts have been developed for recreational use; boardwalks have been constructed, and tourists can enjoy sightseeing harbour cruises in a variety of craft from *Theodore Tugboat* to the tall ship *Silva*. Today, wooden sailing ships are rare, but every so often the Tall Ships Festival brings in magnificent sailing vessels from distant parts that attract crowds of spectators. Normally, the traffic consists mostly of container ships, naval and coastguard vessels, seasonal cruise ships, harbour tour boats, and private sailboats. For the price of a bus fare, passengers aboard the ferries can get some of the best views of the harbour any day of the week, any time of year.

HARBOUR ISLANDS

Sambro and Devils Islands

At the southwestern approach to Halifax Harbour, the oldest functioning lighthouse in North America stands on Sambro Island, known to Champlain as Sesambre, the name given it by fishers from St. Malo. The lighthouse was built in 1758 to guide shipping past its rocky shoals, but Sambro Island has nevertheless witnessed many shipwrecks. The lighthouse was tended by lightkeepers until 1988 when it became automated. Its huge fresnel lens, now replaced by more modern technology, can be seen in the Maritime Museum of the Atlantic on Halifax's waterfront.

During the American Revolution, Sambro witnessed battles between privateers and the British Navy. The War of 1812 brought an American privateer, the *Young Teazer*, which seized two ships near the lighthouse and escaped with them as far as Chester, where she was intercepted by the British Navy. In both the First and Second World Wars, German U-boats attacked allied shipping near Sambro, with the loss of some vessels.

At the northeastern entrance to the harbour stands the Devils Island lighthouse. The island appears on a French chart of 1711 as Île Verte, but on James Cook's charts it is named Devils Island. It was also formerly known as Wood Island or Rous's Island. Like Sambro Island, it is surrounded by rocky shoals on which many ships have been wrecked, but its first lighthouse was not installed until about 1848. A second lighthouse, built in 1877, is still standing but is no longer operational.

Around 1830, Andrew Henneberry and his family moved to Devils Island. Next came Thomas Edwards and his brothers, and the population increased until, in 1901, there were eighteen houses. At one time there was a school on the island, and a general store. In the 1920s there were twenty-eight families, but they were moved to the mainland during the Battle of the Atlantic in the Second World War, when German U-boats sank allied vessels along the coast.

Nova Scotia folklorist Helen Creighton began to visit the island in the late 1920s, gathering songs and stories from the inhabitants, including Ben Henneberry and Gordon Young. Henneberry supplied songs for Creighton's first book, *Songs and Ballads of Nova Scotia*. Her book *Bluenose Ghosts* is a record of tales of the supernatural, many of which were told to her on Devils Island. The island is now uninhabited, but stories about supernatural experiences persist, and the place is visited from time to time by curious ghost-hunters.

McNabs, Lawlor, and Georges Islands

Three islands protect Halifax's inner harbour: McNabs is the largest, separated from the mainland by Eastern Passage and Lawlor Island. Georges Island lies only a short distance from downtown Halifax.

In the late eighteenth and early nineteenth centuries, ships entering or leaving Halifax Harbour would be greeted by a gruesome sight as they passed McNabs Island. The punishment for serious offences in the British military was hanging, so, as a deterrent to others who might be tempted to resist authority or break the law, the corpses of executed mutineers and deserters were tarred and displayed on gibbets at the end of Maughers Beach. The creaking of the wooden gibbets and the rattling of the chains so disturbed Peter McNab, son of the Peter who had originally bought the island, that one night he went out, cut down the bodies, and demolished the gibbets.

The McNabs named the island, but they were not the first inhabitants. The Mi'kmaq hunted and camped there and continued do so for many years after Europeans came. In the seventeenth century the French established a fishing station on what they called the Île de Chibouctou.

Shortly after establishing Halifax, Governor Edward Cornwallis gave the island to three of his nephews, and it became known as Cornwallis Island. Joshua Maugher was granted the beach which still bears his name for a fishery. In 1782, Halifax businessman Peter McNab bought the whole island from the Cornwallises. He built a summer home, and established tenant farmers who cleared land for agriculture. He gave the island to his son Peter II, who made his home there, with a small community of farmers and fishers.

After Peter II's death, Peter III tried unsuccessfully to sell the whole island. It was later divided up among family members and eventually sold off, partly to the War Department for fortifications, and partly for recreational use. The number of residents decreased over the years, but it became a popular picnic spot, and two pleasure grounds were established—Woolnough's and Findlay's—with music, dancing, and sports that attracted hundreds of visitors to the island.

A lighthouse has stood on Maughers Beach since 1830. One of the lightkeepers was Matthew Lynch, whose son William worked at Findlay's pleasure ground, with its merry-go-round and carnival attractions. William bought the operation and established the Bill Lynch Shows, a popular and long-lived touring carnival.

Several fortifications were built on the island, beginning with Fort Ives. Some were still in use during the Second World War, and the last one ceased operations in 1992. The remains of the forts and batteries can be found on the island, which is now part of a provincial park. Most of the original homes are long gone, but visitors can enjoy the island's hiking trails and historic sites, explore the shoreline, and observe the wildlife and a variety of trees, plants, and flowers.

The island that lies between McNabs and the mainland was acquired by James Lawlor in the early nineteenth century. He established a small farm there, but it was sparsely populated. In 1864, during the American Civil War, Lawlor Island witnessed a dramatic event when the *Talahassee*, a Confederate ship which had been refuelling in the harbour, slipped out through the Eastern Passage to avoid capture by Union ships that were thought (erroneously, as it happened) to be waiting at the entrance to the main channel. The *Talahassee* successfully navigated the shallow waters of the passage and made her escape.

In 1866 the government established a quarantine station there after an outbreak of cholera, brought to the city on an incoming vessel. Hospitals and a disinfection building had been constructed by the end of the century, with a cemetery on the northern tip of the island. In 1899, immigrants from Russia, led by Count Sergius Tolstoy, son of author Leo Tolstoy, were housed there for a short time when an outbreak of smallpox was feared on their vessel. Improved preventive health measures rendered the quarantine station redundant by 1938, and during the Second World War the island was used as a government medical facility.

Today, there are no buildings on the island, and it is part of the McNabs and Lawlor Island Provincial Park, being kept as a nature reserve and not open to the public.

Georges Island, topped by its fort, lies closest to the Halifax shore. It was frequented by the Mi'kmaq and by French fishers. The French called it Île Raquette, or Île Ronde, and for many years they dried fish on its shores. In 1746, it became the burial place for the ill-fated duc d'Anville. His body was later transferred to Louisbourg.

When Halifax was founded in 1749, the British named the island in honour of King George II. Many of the first settlers disembarked there, living in tents while they worked on clearing the forest and building the town. Once they were settled on the mainland, the island was fortified with earthworks and a palisade as part of the harbour's defences. Storage sheds were built and were soon used as prisons for those convicted of anything from petty crime to murder.

When the Foreign Protestants arrived in the harbour, many of them were set to work on the construction of the island's fortifications, in order to pay off the expenses of their voyage. They lived in cramped and uncomfortable barracks until the following year when they were moved to the mainland, and eventually, in 1753, to Lunenburg.

Georges Island's prisons were used by Governor Lawrence in 1755 to house a delegation of Acadian deputies who came to Halifax to negotiate an agreement of neutrality, instead of signing an unconditional oath of allegiance to the British Crown. They were unsuccessful and were imprisoned and then deported along with hundreds of other Acadians.

With the outbreak of the Seven Years' War between England and France, in 1756, the defences of Georges Island were augmented, and the prisons were filled with men from captured French ships. In the early 1760s they also housed Acadian partisans led by Joseph Broussard, along with other rebels who had escaped deportation.

The American Revolution brought further additions to the fortifications, and troops were stationed in a new barracks. The Naval Hospital was relocated to the island, and ships coming into harbour stopped to disembark the wounded. The island was also used several times in the eighteenth century as a quarantine station. It was the scene of a grizzly punishment in 1785 when two pirates were hanged and their bodies covered with tar and exhibited on gibbets.

Changes came about with the arrival of Prince Edward, who had a star-shaped fort constructed on the island. Named Fort Charlotte, after the queen, it formed

Fort Charlotte, Georges Island, ca. 1876.

part of the prince's telegraphic communication system from the harbour entrance to the Citadel. The prince also built a new military hospital on the island, which lasted until a Martello tower and other buildings were constructed in 1812. By the 1860s, the fortifications had deteriorated, and the island's defences were once again updated, with new buildings and underground tunnels. Married quarters were established in 1871, Fort Charlotte was improved, and from 1873 to 1906 Georges Island served as a base for assembling and deploying mines. The Martello tower was dismantled in 1877.

Surprisingly, it was not until 1876, after many ships had run aground on the island, that a wooden lighthouse was built with an attached house for the lightkeeper. It was destroyed by fire in 1916 and replaced by the taller concrete structure that stands today.

In 1914 Fort Charlotte once again served as a military base and the defences were modernized. At the end of the war, the fort was closed and the island virtually abandoned. The Second World War saw the installation of anti-aircraft guns, although they were never put to use. Since then, there has been no military presence on the island.

The tunnels built under the island's fortifications have been a source of curiosity for many years, as it was said that they were linked to tunnels on the mainland, designed to allow escape from the Citadel should it come under attack from the land. No underwater tunnels have been found to date, but the story persists and the question remains open.

Today, the island and fort are recognized as a National Historic Site, restored and maintained by Parks Canada, which runs tours for the public from time to time. It is well worth a visit.

BEDFORD BASIN

The Narrows at the northern end of Halifax Harbour opens into Bedford Basin, where the historic Princes Lodge Rotunda overlooks the water on the western shore. The head of the Basin lies at the mouth of the Sackville River, one of the routes used by the Mi'kmaq to reach K'jipuktuk. They lived in the coves where fish and molluscs were plentiful. An area called the Bedford Barrens has been designated a National Historic Site, because of the special significance of this area to the Mi'kmaq, as evidenced by petroglyphs carved into the rock.

The arrival of European fishing boats and the early colonial disputes between France and England seem not to have interrupted the Indigenous Peoples' use of the area. In 1746, the remains of a fleet of ships led by the duc d'Anville limped through the Narrows and set up camp on the shore near Birch Cove. Disease had spread among the seamen, some of whom died there. D'Anville, too, died shortly after they arrived. The survivors had no alternative but to return to France, leaving behind a few sunken vessels. They also left devastation among the Mi'kmaq who had no immunity to the sickness brought by the French. Many died, and disease spread among the wider Mi'kmaw population; it is said that hundreds more died in the following months.

When Cornwallis arrived in 1749, he built Fort Sackville as part of Halifax's outer defences at the head of what was initially called Torrington Bay, and later became known as Bedford Basin, in honour of the Duke of Bedford. The road leading to the fort and onward to Windsor ran along the Basin's western shore. In 1767 Joseph Scott, a Halifax merchant, acquired a large grant of land beside the fort, where he built his home. It survives today as the Scott Manor House and serves as a museum. Later, Scott built an inn beside the road, called Ten Mile House, that has also survived, though it is no longer an inn. From these beginnings, the town of Bedford grew up.

When Prince Edward, Duke of Kent, was posted to Halifax at the end of the eighteenth century, he lived with his mistress, Julie St-Laurent, at Princes Lodge on a property on the western side of the Basin provided by Governor John Wentworth. The round building, in the classical style, that still sits on a knoll overlooking the Basin was built by the Prince as a place of quiet recreation for himself and Julie.

Other comfortable rural retreats owned by prosperous merchants had a view of the water. In the early nineteenth century there were several inns and some industries—gristmills, sawmills, tanneries, a paper mill, and a woollen mill—along the road on the western shore, and ships were built at the head of the Basin. In 1855, the Nova Scotia Railway opened a line from Halifax's Richmond station, running beside the Basin between the highway and the shore. A causeway was built, using huge loads of rock, to carry the tracks across Mill Cove, earning it the name of Duncan's Dump, thought to be derived from the name of the contractor.

Later in the nineteenth century, some of the big estates on the west side of the Basin were broken up. The area was increasingly used for recreation, and the shores of the Basin became "cottage country" for citizens of Halifax, who travelled out of the city by train to Rockingham station and other minor stopping places along the route. Summer cottages were built and hotels accommodated both travellers and holiday-makers. Day-trippers from Halifax came by train, in search of swimming and sailing in summer, and skating in winter.

In the mid-nineteenth century, a small Black village grew up on Fairview Cove at the southern end of the Basin, where formerly Mi'kmaw wigwams had stood. The Campbell Road Community eventually came to be known as Africville. It was a vibrant and close-knit community, where residents took pride in their houses, their kinship, and their church. Over time, a prison, a garbage dump, an abattoir, a hospital for infectious diseases, and a fertilizer plant were all established nearby, and Africville's neglected residents lacked services such as water, sewage, and public transport. Civic officials claimed it was a slum, and in the 1960s, in spite of protest by the homeowners and meetings with city officials, the homes were destroyed and the residents relocated. Today, Africville (formerly Seaview) Park, and a replica of the church that serves as a museum, overlook the Basin and keep the community's collective memory alive.

The Basin was used during the First World War as anchorage for vessels preparing to leave in convoys with supplies for Britain. Large numbers of ships assembled there before being marshalled into groups that would leave Halifax under naval escort. The only way out of the Basin was through the Narrows, and despite a

Ships assembled in Bedford Basin, preparing to cross the Atlantic Ocean under naval escort in the Second World War.

system of controls, the Halifax Explosion was perhaps an accident waiting to happen. The destruction extended into the south end of the Basin, including Africville, where damage was sustained to people and property. The Mi'kmaw settlement at Turtle Grove at the northern end of the Narrows was completely destroyed, and many of its residents were killed.

During the Second World War, convoys once again formed in the Bedford Basin before heading across the Atlantic, escorted by vessels of the Canadian Navy. In 1945, just after the end of the war in Europe, a fire broke out in the Bedford Magazine on the eastern side, causing a series of explosions which resulted in understandable panic in the surrounding communities. However, damage was far less than in 1917 and there were very few injuries and only one fatality.

During the twentieth century, the shores of the Bedford Basin became a residential area, with private homes, apartments, shops, motels, and restaurants. The town of Bedford has grown considerably and at the time of writing has a population of around thirty-five thousand. Today, large vessels load and unload at Halifax's second container port in Fairview Cove. The Bedford Institute of Oceanography lies on the eastern shore, and a barge moored in the Basin conducts research into sonar and other marine apparatus.

The Basin is no longer cottage country, but it is still used for recreational purposes. The Bedford Basin Yacht Club was established in the 1950s at Summer Cove, and warm weather brings many sailboats and other craft out onto the water.

THE NORTHWEST ARM

People driving in or out of Halifax past the head of the Northwest Arm in summer will see a great many pleasure boats, either moored or under sail. Its shores are home to several yacht clubs, as well as private wharves and public parks. But it was not always a recreational area; it has seen fisheries, industries, and prisons. Today, a tower rises above the trees, with its own story to tell.

The Arm, as its name suggests, branches northwest out of the harbour and thus forms the peninsula on which the city of Halifax was built. It was thought by the first British settlers to be a river, known as either Hawke's or Sandwich River. It is in fact a drowned river valley, with small brooks emptying into it at various points. The Mi'kmaq named it Wagwoltichk (spellings vary), meaning "the end of the bay," and the name is used today for the Waegwoltic Club on the southeast side. Cornwallis's settlers soon established a sawmill on the brook dropping down from Indian (now Chocolate) Lake, but this met with resistance from the Mi'kmaq, who raided the mill, killing some of the workers. A blockhouse was built overlooking the head of the Arm to ensure security.

Fortifications at Point Pleasant began in the 1760s to protect Halifax from attack by sea. For some years, a chain boom extended across the Arm from a rock at Point Pleasant, to prevent enemy ships from entering and invading Halifax from the rear.

Towards the end of the eighteenth century, land on the Arm was granted for farming and fishing, and settlement began along the shore. Industrial development increased in the nineteenth century when the sawmill site at the head of the Arm became in turn a chocolate mill (giving its name to the lake) and a gristmill, operated by John Hosterman. The same brook powered a snuff mill, and later a foundry. Near the end of the nineteenth century, the Hosterman enterprise had collapsed, except for a nail factory, but several small industries took over the site, including a paint company, whose premises burned down in 1877, and a barite mill that survived into the twentieth century. A second mill was powered by the brook that came down from Williams Lake. Originally a gristmill, it later produced other commodities. Meanwhile, quarries on the western shore supplied ironstone, granite, and slate for fortifications and road building.

From early days of settlement, fishing boats set out from the Arm, where fish lots were laid out in the 1760s. Wharves and fish sheds were built along the shore below Williams Lake, and there was another fishery on the eastern shore.

The 1800s saw the establishment of several grand estates on the peninsula side, developed by Halifax's elite who escaped from the congestion and smells of the commercial city to enjoy the clean air of what was then country. They were occupied by businessmen, politicians, judges, and other dignitaries, many of whose names are familiar to Nova Scotians. Belmont was the birthplace of Joseph Howe, while Sir Samuel Cunard's son William lived at Oaklands, the Hon. David M. McKeen at Maplewood, and retired Judge John William Ritchie at Belmont. Over the years, these estates were broken up, mostly giving way to housing in the twentieth century. Many of their names are preserved in the surrounding streets. Surprisingly, not far from these estates, the Northwest Arm Penitentiary was built in 1844, near Point Pleasant Park.

Over the years, several ferries have carried passengers across the Arm. In the nineteenth century, boats crossed from the foot of Jubilee Road to Melville Island, while others ran from Quinpool and Oakland Roads. The longest-lasting one was established by the Purcell family in 1853. It carried passengers between Point Pleasant Park and Purcells Cove for 118 years. More recently, a ferry service was initiated to avoid traffic congestion while work was carried out on a road leading out of Halifax.

Several clubs providing recreational facilities were established during the early twentieth century on the Northwest Arm, and boating and swimming became popular pastimes. Now, in the warmer months of the year, all kinds of craft, from paddleboards, canoes, racing skiffs and small sailboats, to ocean-going yachts, can be seen on the water.

Two large parks lie on either side of the Arm: Point Pleasant, with the remains of its fortifications, and Fleming Park, known as the Dingle. This was the former home of Sir Sandford Fleming, who built the Intercolonial Railway and introduced standard time to Canada. He donated the property to Haligonians in 1908. At his instigation, the tower that overlooks the water, now called Sir Sandford Fleming Memorial Tower, was constructed to commemorate the introduction of representative government to Nova Scotia.

Melville and Deadmans Islands

Melville Island, situated in a cove near the head of the Arm, and now home to the Armdale Yacht Club, has a grim history. It was first granted to Robert Cowie and John Aubony in 1752 and later acquired by John Kavanagh for his fishery, whereupon it became known as Kavanaghs Island.

During the French Revolution, some French sailors were taken prisoner and housed in Kavanagh's fish stores, but in the Napoleonic Wars a larger facility was needed for French captives. A prison was built in 1803 consisting of a large wooden structure overlooked by a stone officers' house. At about the same time, the island was renamed for the newly appointed First Lord of the Admiralty, Henry Dundas, Viscount Melville.

The prison inmates lived relatively well, making crafts for sale to nearby residents, practising their trades, or working outside the prison. Inevitably, some tried to escape, and if caught they were subject to confinement in what was known as the Black Hole. Prisoners who died were buried on Deadmans Island, adjacent to Melville Island, and joined to the mainland by a narrow strip of land.

When war broke out with the Americans in 1812, most of the French prisoners were either paroled or moved out of the area, and replaced by Americans, many of them privateers. Their numbers quickly grew as their vessels were seized, and they lived in poor conditions because of overcrowding. The winters were cold, fuel was scarce, and disease was rife. The prisoners were subject to epidemics, and by the time news of the end of the war reached Melville Island in 1815, nearly two hundred Americans had died and were buried on Deadmans Island.

The surviving Americans were eventually released and their places taken by a contingent of Black refugees who had escaped from slavery during the war. They were housed in the refurbished prison building while waiting to receive land grants. Then the buildings lay vacant for a time, but in 1818 the island was used as a quarantine hospital for smallpox victims from an immigrant ship. It continued in use from time to time to avoid the spread of disease from incoming vessels. The last occasion was an outbreak of typhus in 1847. Once again, the dead were interred on Deadmans Island.

In 1855, the old prison building became a barracks for American volunteers recruited to serve in the Crimean War. It was next used by the British as a military prison until the early twentieth century. It came under Canadian control in 1905 when the British military relinquished its responsibilities in Canada. A stone military prison was constructed alongside the old wooden structure, a house was built for the chief warder, and in 1909 the island became a Canadian military detention barracks. During the First World War it housed some captured German reservists and suspect aliens living in Nova Scotia.

A fire destroyed the old wooden building in 1935, and with the outbreak of the Second World War, military detainees were removed and the island was used for ammunition storage. After the war it was sold to the Armdale Yacht Club, which occupies it today. The Chief Warder's house is now the clubhouse, and the former prison building is used for storage.

Meanwhile, in 1907, Deadmans Island was sold to Charles F. Longley, who established an amusement park with a children's playground, a pavilion with a dance hall, and various forms of entertainment. The park and pavilion closed in 1927, only to change hands and reopen three years later. "Melville Park" closed permanently in 1938.

Deadmans Island was spared from development after it had been determined that up to four hundred burials had taken place there, and in 2000 a park was established by Halifax Regional Municipality to commemorate the dead. US servicemen conducted a service in memory of nearly two hundred of their fellow citizens whose bodies rest there, and in 2005 a memorial was installed by the United States Government. The island is now a quiet, secluded park overlooking the Northwest Arm.

South Shore

ST. MARGARETS BAY

Peggys Cove

This exploration of Nova Scotia's harbours continues by following the Lighthouse Route, leading out of Halifax towards St. Margarets Bay and the village of Peggys Cove. Tucked among granite rocks scraped bare by glaciers, this picturesque fishing village lies at the eastern entrance to the bay, which extends between the Chebucto and Aspotogan Peninsulas. Of all the beautiful, rocky inlets within a short drive of Halifax, Peggys Cove is the best-known.

The much-photographed lighthouse perched on granite rocks, and the fishing boats in its enclosed harbour make Peggys Cove a popular destination. The cove's earliest residents would be astonished by the busloads of cruise-ship passengers who are disgorged onto the parking lots to swarm over the rocks during summer and early fall. Once known as Eastern Point Harbour or Peggs Harbour, the origin of the name is shrouded in mystery; some accounts link it to St. Margarets Bay ("Peggy" being a nickname for Margaret), others to the wife of an early settler. A more romantic story is that a woman named Peggy was the sole survivor of a shipwreck, and she lived in the cove and married a local resident.

By the early twentieth century the population of the village had grown to about three hundred, with houses scattered on the rocky ground on both sides of the harbour. The residents were mostly fishers, or employed in fish processing. In addition to the lobster cannery, there were flakes for drying salt cod. There was also a school and a general store. St John's Anglican Church, built in the 1890s, is still in use.

The iconic lighthouse was built in 1868, to guide shipping safely into St. Margarets Bay. For many years it was operated as a post office, and visitors enjoyed sending postcards with the distinctive postmark that included the lighthouse image.

Artist William deGarthe made his summer home in the cove and began a career of portraying scenes from village life, in particular the lives of fishers in the twentieth century. He also carved the Fishermen's Memorial Monument on the rock face near his house, honouring the local families. This ten-year project was incomplete at the time of his death, but was completed by another artist who had worked with him during the first five years.

Although the permanent population of the village has shrunk to about thirty, there are still full-time fishers using the wharves. The Peggy's Cove Commission oversees the preservation of the village's character by careful regulation, so visitors today can see the harbour and the cluster of homes around it much as they would have been one hundred years ago.

Little Harbours on the Bay

The journey continues around the bay past other scenic harbours. Many centuries ago, these inlets were havens for transient European fishers. Settlement began in the area in the latter part of the eighteenth century with the Dauphinees and the Boutiliers, whose roots were in Montbéliard, France. They came from Lunenburg to a cove on the eastern side of the bay with a wide view across the water that became known as French Village. Families spread out from there, leaving their names in the fishing villages around the bay. In 1794, James Frederick Boutilier and his cousin John Coulaw Boutilier bought land at what came to be known as Boutiliers Point, naming the nearby harbour of Cowlow Cove. Other family members settled on the east side of the bay, at Boutiliers Cove.

Brothers John and Frederick Dauphinee moved across the bay to the harbour that is now Hubbards, giving their name to Dauphinees Beach and Dauphinees Point. The village that grew up there was called Hibberts Cove, said to be named after Hibbert Dauphinee, and later known as Hubbards. Its residents caught and processed fish, and cut lumber. Today, Hubbards is a growing community that welcomes visitors, especially for festive lobster suppers.

Fishing was the chief occupation of all the villages around the bay for many generations but in the twentieth century, the younger generations started to move away to find work in cities. Several older homes became summer cottages for people from Halifax, who might come and stay for all of June and July. There were train stations serving French Village, St. Margarets Bay, Ingramport, and Hubbards, so it was not uncommon for men to commute daily, or perhaps just on Friday and Monday. Eventually cars replaced trains, and today an increasing number of people live at the head of the bay and work in Halifax. Fishing boats still work out of small

Washing nets at Northwest Cove in 1956.

harbours from Northwest Cove to Peggys Cove, and lobster has replaced cod and mackerel as the most important catch.

On the opposite side of the bay, Northwest Cove is also a long-established fishing harbour. Less well-known than Peggys Cove, it has a similar history of settlement. It shared with Peggys Cove the effects of a major disaster that took place in St. Margarets Bay in 1998. Just after 10:30 p.m. on September 2, when most of the residents had gone to bed, they were startled by a loud boom out on the water, followed by the sound of sirens. A passenger plane, Swissair 111, travelling from New York to Geneva, was in trouble. The pilot had hoped to make an emergency landing in Halifax, but the plane came down in the water at the entrance to the bay.

Word quickly spread that a plane had crashed and local fishers from all around the bay, who were accustomed to looking out for their colleagues at sea, quickly set out in their boats in a vain search for survivors. They were unprepared for the devastating scene of wreckage they found. In the following days and weeks, residents from all around the bay were involved in supporting the teams whose gruesome task was the retrieval of the remains of the plane and its 229 passengers. They were also there to help the relatives of the victims who flew in from many parts of the world. The disaster had a profound emotional effect on many people in the communities around St. Margarets Bay.

Stark granite memorials have been erected on each side of the entrance to the bay, looking towards the spot where the tragedy took place. Today, visitors to these quiet places recall the greatest disaster in St. Margarets Bay's history.

MAHONE BAY

The scenic route continues around Mahone Bay, between the Aspotogan Peninsula and Lunenburg. There are numerous islands in this bay—said to be as many as there are days in the year, although this is a generous estimate. The name Mahone may come from the French word *mahonne*, referring to a type of boat apparently favoured by pirates who lurked among the islands to attack passing vessels. For hundreds of years there were Mi'kmaw communities on islands and inlets all along the coast, and today there is a reserve at Gold River, part of the Acadia First Nation.

Today, there are small communities around the bay, the two largest of which are Chester and the town of Mahone Bay.

Chester

Chester is a charming little community blessed with two harbours. What is known locally as "the peninsula" is in fact an island, joined to the village by a narrow causeway that leads to some of the most expensive properties in the area.

The town plan was laid out by Jonathan Prescott in about 1760 for settlers from New England. He combined his skills as a surveyor and a surgeon and became captain of the Chester militia. Prescott and another man, Benjamin Bridge, were already established in the area when the first New Englanders arrived.

The newcomers were welcomed, both by these residents and by the local Mi'kmaq, who danced for their entertainment on the first evening, bringing food and items to sell. A journal kept by the Rev. John Seccombe, one of the community leaders, tells of a Mi'kmaw woman bringing five salmon and eight salmon trout in a birchbark canoe. "One of the salmon weighed twenty-two pounds and one dozen of the trout weighed fourteen pounds." Indigenous hunters continued to supply the new residents with partridge, moose, bear, and other items. Mi'kmaw women brought sealskins for sale, and on one occasion traded mink pelts and a large bearskin for a quart of wine.

By 1763, thirty families were living in Chester. They cleared land for homes and gardens, but the soil was unsuitable for extensive agriculture, and they made their living by fishing and lumbering. Soon, fifty families had settled, and two sawmills were operating. Fishers based in Chester's harbours sold cod, salmon, and mackerel. The fishery, boat building, lumbering, and the export of forest products were the main occupations for many years.

During the American Revolution, privateering took place around Chester and elsewhere in the bay. In 1776, a Chester schooner, the *Patty*, was captured by an American vessel and taken away with a local boy on board. In 1782, three American privateers entered the harbour and fired at the town. The militia's guns were unable to deter them and the crews landed, ostensibly seeking permission to bury their dead. Jonathan Prescott became suspicious and invited the schooner captains to his house to discuss arrangements. While they were there, Prescott's son knocked on the door, asking loudly where he might billet a hundred Lunenburg militiamen. He was told to put them in Houghton's barn, ready for an assault in the morning. The ruse was effective, and the privateers, thinking they would be outnumbered, made a discreet withdrawal.

More privateering occurred during the War of 1812, and in 1813 the American privateer *Young Teazer* was pursued into Mahone Bay having escaped from an encounter with British ships at the mouth of Halifax Harbour. After a long chase among the islands, the vessel ran aground on Quaker Island, off Chester Harbour. She was fired on by guns on shore, and the captain realized that the game was up. One of the ship's officers, a deserter from the British navy, knew that he would be hanged if he was caught. To avoid capture, he set fire to the powder magazine, and the vessel exploded in a sheet of flame. He and many of his shipmates were killed, and of the eight survivors, most were severely injured.

The story does not end there. Local historian Mather Byles DesBrisay wrote, "A superstition has arisen amongst the inhabitants of the islands in Chester Bay, that the *Teazer*, like the *Flying Dutchman* of old, supernaturally visits the waters in which she met her fate, and that the '*Teazer* light' has long been a matter of alarm to many while passing over Chester Bay." Tales of the fiery ghost ship are still told in local communities.

A grand regatta was held in September 1856, attended by over three thousand people. Races were held for various types of craft, and the day ended, according to DesBrisay, with "general illumination, fine torchlight procession, and a beautiful

This sawmill on the Mushamush River provided lumber for shipbuilders.

display of fireworks." A few years later, a ladies' race was held, with two crews of four—but the coxswains were both male. The day finished with a ball in honour of the winners. These events would develop into today's annual Chester Race Week, Canada's largest regatta, which attracts visiting sailors, including some from New England, who gather there for four days of keelboat racing.

The Tancook ferry leaves from Chester, carrying passengers to and from the island several times a day. The yacht club attracts visiting mariners as well as the local population, and two boatyards offer maintenance, mooring, and storage facilities. The Lordly House Museum provides a glimpse into Chester's history, and other interesting old buildings have attracted filmmakers in search of an old-world setting. There is a vibrant arts community, with a theatre presenting live performances and an art centre focusing on painting.

Town of Mahone Bay

The view of three churches standing side by side at the head of Mahone Bay is one of the most famous in this area. The town itself has many art galleries, restaurants, and gift shops which invite visitors to linger and enjoy the scenery.

Before European settlement was established in 1754, the Mi'kmaq resided on the Mushamush River, at Indian Point, and in the surrounding area. Several

German families came from Lunenburg to clear the farm lots they had been granted. Among them were Peter Zwicker and his family, who built the first house in the community on the west side of the harbour. The Zwickers' son, Peter II, inherited the farm, and became prosperous. Johann Christian Ernst received a farm lot on the east side of the harbour, where he and his wife built a house on the hill overlooking the bay and raised their thirteen children. In 1777, the English Kedy brothers, Alexander and William, bought a sawmill on the Mushamush River at the head of the bay, along with mill lands. Peter Zwicker's grandson George bought a second mill and lands farther south, along the Ernst Brook. His house, now a café, and the Kedy house are the oldest surviving houses in the town.

Although the original settlers came from farming backgrounds, they soon adapted to working in the fishery and merchant shipping. The first shipyards were established by two of Peter Zwicker's great-grandsons and by Christian Ernst's grandson Jacob. Shipbuilding soon became the community's main occupation, with over five hundred vessels launched during the nineteenth century. Some of them became part of the Lunenburg fishing fleet, while trading vessels sailed away with loads of salt fish and lumber, bringing back sugar, molasses and, of course, rum. As well as building ships with wood from their own mill, the Ernst family operated fishing schooners and merchant vessels. They ran a store which was stocked with goods brought in from Halifax and more distant ports.

During the American Revolution, the community attracted the attention of privateers, who raided the town, seizing a vessel and her cargo. Legends of piracy abound in this area, and the *"Teazer* light" is said to appear here, too, from time to time.

The Zwicker Inn on the west side of the harbour provided entertainment for travellers. It received distinguished guests when the family of Lieutenant-Governor Lord Dalhousie spent a pleasant vacation there in summer of 1818. The accommodation was primitive but, he reported, "[T]he Zwickers have been most obliging and kind, anxious in the extreme to do anything in their power to serve them."

By the end of the nineteenth century, the community was flourishing, but with the end of the age of sail the economy suffered. During Prohibition, fishers turned to the more lucrative business of rum-running. Today, the harbour is busy with recreational craft, and the Heritage Boat Yard maintains the community's shipbuilding tradition.

The Mahone Bay Museum on the main street tells the story of the town's foundation and development. In the quiet cemetery, the inscriptions on the earliest gravestones, carved in German and using the old German script, commemorate the first families. The Heritage Boat Yard Co-op Festival celebrates Mahone Bay's shipbuilding and sea-going history. Other festivals through the year make this a lively and attractive community, remembering the past while making the most of the present.

The Tancooks

From Chester, a ferry takes residents and visitors to and from the two Tancook Islands towards the eastern entrance to the bay. Big Tancook, the largest of Mahone Bay's islands, was originally named Queen Charlotte's Island, but this was changed to a derivation from the Mi'kmaw word K'tancook, thought to mean "facing out to sea." The island was settled by families from Lunenburg starting in 1797, and by 1829, there were thirty families living there. By the 1880s the population stood at about five hundred, mostly descendants of the original settlers. There was a Baptist church, and by 1895 there were a hundred and twenty children attending the island school. The early residents were farmers, and they were well-known for growing fine cabbages, some of which were exported, while some were used to produce sauerkraut, for which the island became famous.

In the nineteenth century, fishing and boat building were integral parts of the economy. In particular, the island was known for its Tancook Whalers, sturdy schooners with a good turn of speed that were used for fishing by locals as well as mainlanders. Before a regular ferry service was established, the islands were reached either by private boat, or in winter, on foot across the ice.

Big Tancook's population declined during the twentieth century, and only about a hundred and twenty people now live there year-round, though in summer this number almost doubles. Deer from the mainland have destroyed the cabbage farms, and the sauerkraut factory has moved to the mainland along with the boatyard. Today, the residents' vegetable gardens are securely fenced to keep out the deer. Lobster fishing brings in a good income, but once the season is over, there are more pleasure craft than fishing vessels moored at the wharf, and the summer visitors help to sustain the economy.

The ferry brings tourists to the island, takes commuters to the mainland to work, and takes high school students across to complete their education. A handful of younger children attend the island's one-room school, one of the last remaining in Canada. Many young people have left Big Tancook, but some older folks have come back here to retire, and summer residents still enjoy the slow, quiet way of life.

Little Tancook, the second largest island in the bay, has a similar story. The Levy family were the original settlers, and a handful of their descendants have stayed on the island. Like its larger neighbour, it is served by the ferry from Chester, which also takes younger children to school on the bigger island. Today, about two dozen people live there year-round, and the number is augmented by summer residents.

Not far from Big Tancook's harbour is tiny Star Island, said to have been frequented by pirates and privateers in the late seventeenth and eighteenth centuries. It is particularly associated with the pirate Edward Baker. He is reputed to have stashed two hundred thousand dollars in gold and other goods on the island, but no one has ever admitted to finding it.

East Ironbound

Beyond the Tancooks lies the remote, rocky island of East Ironbound at the entrance to the bay. Its lighthouse is well positioned to guide coastal shipping. The first structure, built in 1867, was struck by lightning three years later and replaced by the present lighthouse and lightkeeper's house. Although the light is now automated, the buildings have been preserved as examples of the combined light and dwelling that were once found in may places along the coast.

In the 1920s, author Frank Parker Day spent some time on the island, using it as the setting for his novel *Rockbound*. His depiction of family strife within this isolated community offended the residents of East Ironbound and aroused controversy, but the book remained popular and remains in print.

Oak Island

Probably the best-known of Mahone Bay's islands is Oak Island, famous for the treasure pit where the notorious pirate Captain Kidd is supposed to have buried his ill-gotten loot. Lying between Western Shore and Martins Point, today the island is joined to the mainland by a causeway, but for many years, residents and treasure-hunters went there by boat.

The island was first settled in the 1760s by New Englanders, among them John McMullen, Daniel McInnis, James McInnes, Enos Jodrey, and Edward Smith. It was known as Smith's Island for some years. Samuel Ball, a Black Loyalist who had been a slave in South Carolina, came there during the American Revolution and operated a thirty-six-acre farm with his wife, Mary.

Another man named Smith, who had come to the island as a boy, was among those who first explored what was reputed to be Captain Kidd's treasure pit. According to Judge DesBrisay, in the late 1700s, Daniel McInnis came upon an area on John Smith's land that had previously been cleared of oak trees except for one, where an old block and tackle had been installed. A hollow in the ground beneath the block suggested that it had been disturbed at some previous time.

Legend had it that a former member of Kidd's pirate crew had said on his deathbed that he had participated in burying a huge sum of money on an island "east of Boston." Numerous unsuccessful attempts had been made to find it. With this story in mind, Smith, McInnis, and Anthony Vaughn Jr. set about exploring the site. They found a layer of flagstones about two feet down, and below that an old clay-lined pit about seven feet across, that had been filled with loose soil, and ten feet further down, a layer of oak logs. They continued to dig another fifteen feet until they could go no further, at which point they stopped.

Some fifteen years later the three returned with others for a second attempt. This time they went deeper and found another layer of logs, below that some charcoal, then putty, then a stone with an undecipherable inscription. At the depth of about ninety feet, the pit began to take in water. This was to be the story of future explorations undertaken in 1848, 1861, 1863, and into the 1890s. DesBrisay's account ends with an attempt in 1893, by which time every digging was followed by a cave-in.

Many subsequent attempts have been made to solve the mystery of what some still believe to be Kidd's money pit. Alternative theories attribute the treasure to Blackbeard, to other notorious pirates, or to the Knights Templar. Somewhere along the line, the tale grew up that a curse was attached to the pit. Nevertheless, huge amounts of money have been invested in fruitless searches, all of which have ended in failure, defeated by the incoming water.

Today, a tourist resort operates on part of the privately owned island. The Friends of Oak Island offer tours, and the Oak Island Interpretation Centre gives visitors a glimpse of the island's history. The mystery of Captain Kidd's treasure remains to be solved.

LUNENBURG BAY AND LAHAVE RIVER

The road westward from Mahone Bay leads to Lunenburg Bay and the LaHave River, sites of the earliest French settlement on the Atlantic coast. It was here that an enduring alliance was forged between the French and the Mi'kmaq. Here, too, some of the earliest British settlement took place.

Lunenburg

Lunenburg Bay and Harbour have sheltered craft of all kinds, from Mi'kmaw canoes to the many fishing vessels that have made this their home port. At one time, every little cove from Eastern Points to Kingsburg had fishing boats moored at its wharves. These waters also saw pirates and privateers, rum-runners, and gold rush speculators. Times have changed: tourism has become a major industry, and many of the boats using the harbour are pleasure craft.

Lunenburg Bay's recorded history goes back to the seventeenth century, although it was home to the Mi'kmaq from as long as ten thousand years ago. They called it Merligueche, which has been interpreted in different ways but may mean "whitecaps that topped the waves." Before the colonial period, as in other parts of Mi'kma'ki, the people hunted animals for the food they needed, using every part of each creature that they killed—bones, skin, sinew, meat—and they gathered plants and fruits, freshwater and saltwater fish, as well as shellfish. They established a portage route between the bay and the LaHave River, which is now a paved road named Indian Path Road.

The first Frenchman known to have come to Merligueche was Nicolas Denys, an entrepreneur who had arrived in Acadie in 1632 with a colonizing expedition led by Isaac de Razilly. He set up a lumber camp in the oak forest on the western shore of the bay, where he produced planks, beams, and barrel staves for export to France, and probably employed some Mi'kmaw workers. He certainly employed their children to pick berries for him.

Razilly and some companions came by boat from LaHève to visit his lumber camp one memorable day. As they sailed into Merligueche Bay, they passed a small, rocky island. Denys tells this story:

> I was in this bay with Monsieur de Razilly and some Indian guides, and as we passed this island an interpreter told us that the Indians never set foot there. When we asked him why, he replied that according to the Indians, when a man set foot on this island, his private parts would immediately catch fire and burn. This made us laugh, even more when Commander de Razilly told a Capuchin father who was more than sixty years old to go there to disabuse those people of their error, and he refused and would not do so whatever Monsieur de Razilly said to him.

They went on to enjoy a magnificent feast at Denys's lumber camp, but these pleasant times were not to last. This potentially successful business ended when Razilly died in 1636, and Denys was no longer allowed to ship lumber on returning supply vessels. In 1701, his great-nephew, Simon Denys de Bonnaventure, came to the bay and found the site where Denys had been working. He found several piles of abandoned lumber, mostly rotten or riddled with holes.

Two Acadian families, the Guédrys and the Petitpas, came to live on the harbour some time in the mid-seventeenth century and were made to feel welcome by the Mi'kmaq. Their neighbours a little to the north, at Chichimichecaty, were Philippe Mius d'Entremont and his Mi'kmaw wife and their family, who became known simply by the name of Mius. Some of the Guédrys' nine children took Mi'kmaw spouses and thus established an interracial community.

At this time the Acadians and the Mi'kmaq were allied against the British, and the harbour was the scene of at least two confrontations. In 1722, raiding ships from New England seized four families and took them to Boston. They were not held for long, but the people of Merligueche sought their revenge four years later. Members of the Mius and Guédry families, along with their Mi'kmaw families and neighbours, paddled out into the bay and boarded an English merchant vessel. The crew resisted, and some of the raiders fled back to shore, but Jean-Baptiste Guédry, his son, and three of the Mi'kmaq were taken to Boston and hanged for piracy.

There were as many as fifteen families in the area in the 1740s, but as relations with the English colonial authorities became increasingly strained, several Acadians left for French-controlled Île Royale (Cape Breton Island). When Edward Cornwallis visited the harbour in 1749 he observed a few families with "very comfortable wooden houses covered with bark, and a good many cattle and sheep." This was the place where he would establish a new settlement on the northern shore of the harbour.

In early June 1753, fourteen transports sailed in with a contingent of mostly German-speaking settlers who had come to Halifax between 1750 and 1753. These Foreign Protestants—loyal to the King of England—were brought to the newly laid-out town that would now be known as Lunenburg. By this time, only one Acadian, Paul Guédry, remained there. He was known as Old Labrador, probably a corruption of the name LaVerdure by which the family was sometimes known. Today, the only reminder of the former Acadian presence is the Old French Cemetery, where the former inhabitants of Merligueche lie in graves whose wooden crosses have long since rotted away. The Labrador and Mius (spellings vary) families were scattered across Nova Scotia.

Lunenburg town was laid out on a slope facing onto the harbour. For the first few years, the settlers struggled to make a subsistence living and, furthermore, they were let down by the government, having been promised tools and supplies for building their homes and establishing farms. They were also subjected to frequent raids by the Mi'kmaq, who understandably resented the newcomers' intrusion on the land.

Blockhouses and a picket fence were built to defend the town, a fort was built on Battery Point, and a militia was formed. The town slowly began to develop, with simple houses lining the formally laid-out grid of streets. The settlers came from inland areas of Europe and were more used to farming and lumbering than fishing. They were granted farm and forest lots, but within a couple of generations many of Lunenburg's citizens had turned to the sea, and the town's fleet of fishing vessels began to grow.

The American Revolution brought privateering to Lunenburg. In 1780, the Lunenburg militia captured an American brig, the *Sally*, that had anchored off the harbour, and claimed it as a prize with its West Indian cargo of rum, sugar, and molasses. Two years later, Lunenburg was not so lucky. On July 1, six vessels arrived in the harbour with a company of armed rebels who raided the town, looting the houses and shops. Colonel John Creighton, who was manning the blockhouse above the town, was captured and the blockhouse burned. The commander of the privateers demanded a ransom for preserving the town and threatened to burn it if the militia resisted. Lunenburg paid a ransom of £1,000 and the raiders sailed out of the harbour with their plunder, carrying off Creighton and two of his militiamen. A message to Halifax quickly brought an armed naval vessel to Lunenburg, but it arrived too late and the privateers were gone. Their prisoners were taken to New England, and later released. This was not the last visit of privateers, but the defences of Lunenburg were enhanced by the arrival of a detachment of troops and several armed vessels, and with the end of the war, the harassment ceased.

When war broke out again in 1812, preparations were made for renewed privateering. The old defences were in poor shape, and four new blockhouses were built to defend the town. Although trading vessels often travelled in convoys for greater security, one group of Lunenburg ships on their way home from the West Indies was captured by an American privateer, and the cargoes lost. In an effort to recoup these losses, Lunenburg merchants purchased vessels and embarked on their own privateering. Several American ships were captured and brought into port before the war ended.

Throughout the nineteenth century and into the twentieth, the fishery and shipbuilding brought great prosperity to Lunenburg. The town's schooner fleet sailed to the fishing banks off Nova Scotia, to Newfoundland's Grand Banks, and to Labrador. They returned with cargoes of cod that were salted and laid out to dry on flakes along the waterfront before being packed for shipping. Dried salt cod became a major export to Europe and the West Indies. A lighthouse was built in 1864 at Battery Point to guide Lunenburg's vessels into port.

A point at the southern entrance to Lunenburg Bay called The Ovens saw a flurry of excitement in the 1860s when gold was found in seams of quartz in its cliffs and in its sandy beach. The area that had been known until then only for its booming sea caves attracted crowds of prospectors, and a small settlement sprang up that lasted for about ten years, only to vanish again without a trace once the gold was exhausted.

1879, Lunenburg, Nova Scotia. *This bird's-eye view of Lunenburg in the late nineteenth century shows the busy harbour with its wharves and shipping.*

People across Canada carry with them, perhaps unknowingly, a chapter from Lunenburg's history. On the back of every Canadian dime there is an image of the *Bluenose*, a fishing schooner built in 1921 at Lunenburg's Smith and Rhuland yard. She was a working fishing vessel, designed for speed, and is best-known as a prize-winning racing schooner. With Captain Angus Walters at the helm, she won many international races in the 1920s, and continued to win international trophies until just before the Second World War.

In the 1920s some enterprising Lunenburg seamen turned their efforts to rum-running. The best-known of the rum-running vessels was the schooner *I'm Alone*, launched in Lunenburg in 1923 and used by American owners to carry liquor from St. Pierre and Miquelon, and later from the West Indies. Fitted with powerful engines, she appeared by day to be an innocent sailing vessel, but under cover of darkness she could pick up speed to meet her American partners in international waters off the United States. After several narrow escapes, she was sunk in 1929 by the US Coast Guard in the Gulf of Mexico.

In the twentieth century, iron-hulled fishing vessels began to appear along the waterfront. One of the last working schooners, the salt banker *Theresa E. Connor*, is now moored beside the Fisheries Museum of the Atlantic as a reminder of the schooner fleet that once brought prosperity to the town.

Lunenburg's shipyards were busy during both world wars carrying out repairs to naval vessels. During the Second World War, the harbour became the base for the Royal Norwegian Navy, whose vessels had escaped across the Atlantic at the time of the German invasion of Norway.

Fishing and shipbuilding continued in Lunenburg into the post-war years. There was no longer a demand for working schooners, but boats for fishing and pleasure were still required. Several major shipbuilding projects came to Lunenburg, where shipwrights had retained their traditional skills. In 1960, a replica of the square-rigged HMS *Bounty* was launched from the Smith and Rhuland shipyard. In 1963, a replica of the *Bluenose*, known as *Bluenose II*, was commissioned, followed in 1970 by another eighteenth-century replica, HMS *Rose*, which was later used in a movie to represent HMS *Surprise*. *Bluenose II* attracted many tourists as she underwent major restoration in Lunenburg before her re-launching in 2012.

Today, ship repair and maintenance continue on the harbour, and fishing vessels bring their catch to the modern fish-processing plant operated by the Clearwater company just east of the town.

Old Town Lunenburg, with its distinctive architecture and historic waterfront buildings, is recognized as a Canadian National Historic Site and a UNESCO World Heritage Site. The Fisheries Museum of the Atlantic, with historic vessels moored at its wharf, tells the story of the town's fishing community. On the waterfront, beside the old stores and warehouses, stands a memorial to the many Lunenburg fishermen who lost their lives at sea.

LaHave River

The scenic coastal route from Lunenburg leads to the LaHave River. "A river that extends 6 or 7 leagues inland, with little water" was Champlain's description of the LaHave—an unusual error for the great cartographer, who had clearly failed to penetrate beyond the islands at the mouth of the river. Perhaps Messamouet, a Mi'kmaq leader whom he met while his vessel was at anchor in Green Bay, had dissuaded him from encroaching into Indigenous territory.

The LaHave is in fact a major river, once dubbed "the Rhine of Nova Scotia." It runs for nearly one hundred kilometres from the interior of the province to the Atlantic Ocean. It is wide and navigable as far as the head of tide at Bridgewater, with a group of scenic islands at its mouth, and many beautiful coves where fishers and shipbuilders made their livings well into the twentieth century. Many of their descendants still have homes there. Fishing boats still use the river, and the lobster season brings a flurry of activity.

The Mi'kmaq knew the LaHave River well. For thousands of years they travelled along it, camped in its coves, and used the portage route to Merligueche. They probably met and traded with Europeans who sheltered their fishing fleets among the islands early in the sixteenth century.

In May 1604, the Mi'kmaq witnessed the arrival of a French expedition led by Pierre Dugua de Mons, on their way to found a settlement in Acadie. The first headland the French passed as they made landfall reminded them of one that had been their last sight of France. They named it Cap de LaHève, still known today as Cape LaHave, and they named the bay at the entrance to the river Port de LaHève.

Here, the French expedition was greeted by the Indigenous Peoples on the west side of a *petite rivière*, according to Champlain's map of what is now Green Bay. This is probably where Champlain first met Mi'kmaw chief Messamouet, who had previously travelled to France with Basque fishermen. He had stayed at the home of the mayor of Bayonne, could speak French, and would act as Champlain's guide and interpreter in later explorations.

The French moved on, and the Mi'kmaq continued to frequent the area undisturbed. They were joined for a few years in the 1630s by French colonists who farmed the fertile soil around Petite Rivière. Relations between the two communities were good, and some men took Mi'kmaw spouses. Indigenous artifacts have been found around Green Bay, and the local names Indian Pond and Indian Hill attest to Indigenous presence into the time of British settlement. Mi'kmaq still gather annually at their traditional burial ground behind Sperrys Beach, where their ancestors were laid to rest.

LaHave, Riverport, and Bridgewater

The village of LaHave, higher up the river, is the site of the settlement established on Fort Point by French naval officer Isaac de Razilly in September 1632. He arrived with two hundred men, carrying a commission from Louis XIII as his representative in New France. The Mi'kmaq were probably surprised to see his vessels coming to the narrows where two points of land jut out into the river. The men disembarked and unloaded their supplies, including provisions for the winter, livestock, and building materials for a fort and trading post. The passengers included workmen to construct buildings, farmers to cultivate the land, three Capuchin fathers to bring Christianity to the Mi'kmaq, some soldiers, and a few gentlemen. Among them were Razilly's cousin, Charles de Menou d'Aulnay, and merchant Nicolas Denys who was determined to develop the area's natural resources.

The first priority was the construction of Fort Sainte-Marie-de-Grâce, with dwellings for the governor and gentlemen, and living quarters for the workmen. A chapel was built nearby where the Capuchins conducted services and instructed the Mi'kmaq in the basics of Christianity—considered by some to be the earliest school in Canada. A small settlement soon grew up at LaHève. The colonists cultivated gardens, raised livestock and poultry, and planted apple trees. Cattle grazed on the meadow across the river that was known as La Vacherie, behind what is now Oxners Beach. Men were sent to clear land for farms at Petite Rivière. The Mi'kmaq brought beaver pelts to trade for manufactured goods from France.

Supply ships and visiting fishing vessels moored in the lee of the point (now Getsons Cove) and in the larger harbour on the opposite shore (today's Riverport). Incoming ships brought oil, wine, sugar, and other commodities from France, as well as new recruits to the colony. On their return they carried furs and fish, as well as the men whose contracts had expired.

In early summer of 1636, the ship *Saint-Jean* brought a fresh contingent of hopeful immigrants from France, many of them skilled artisans, including some with wives and children. Sadly, the settlement at LaHève ended abruptly shortly thereafter. Razilly died unexpectedly in July, and control passed to Menou d'Aulnay, who transferred most of the settlers to Port Royal. These were the founding families of today's Acadian population.

In the 1760s, New Dublin Township was established on the west side of the LaHave. The town plot was to be on Getsons Cove, near the former fort site, but it was not immediately developed. Instead, the settlement of West LaHave grew up on a brook a little farther upstream, where Joseph Pernette established a farm, a sawmill, and a gristmill. He brought in an English shipwright to build a vessel for exporting lumber. This was the first of many ships built on the LaHave. In the nineteenth century, sawmills and shipyards were operating up and down the river.

Pernette's son John ran a ferry from the shore below the homestead, giving the community the name of West LaHave Ferry. It provided an important link in the Post Road from Lunenburg to Liverpool. John Pernette was required to row the postman and his horse across the river for free, which caused him some annoyance. By about 1900, the ferry across the river was still no more than a rowboat that could carry a horse and a light vehicle. These days, the motorized ferry *Brady Himmelman*, named for a long-time ferry operator, carries cars, recreational vehicles, and heavy trucks between LaHave and East LaHave.

A former ferry about to cross the river with two oarsmen and a passenger's horse and carriage on board, ca. 1900.

West LaHave remained the chief settlement on the river for some years, but soon a fishing village grew up at what is now LaHave. During the nineteenth and early twentieth centuries, most of the area's population was employed in the fishery. There were several processing plants and merchants who exported fish and sold supplies to the fishing schooners and trading ships. The LaHave Outfitting Company was the last of its kind but the premises is now the very popular LaHave Bakery, where travellers and local residents can enjoy a cup of coffee or a meal, visit the art gallery, craft co-op, bookstore, and skateboard business, and where visiting boats can moor. The old building has become a meeting place and cultural centre enjoyed by both residents and visitors.

Fish processing methods changed in the mid-twentieth century, and the flakes for drying cod that lined the shore up to the 1950s were no longer in use. Most fish was stored on ice, processed on shore, and shipped frozen to consumer markets. With the 1990s moratorium on cod, the catch became diversified. Today, many local fishers focus on lobster or on scallop-dragging.

Out on the point, the ruins of the old fort were rapidly disappearing by the early nineteenth century as the cliff was being lost to erosion, and nothing remains of it today. A lighthouse built nearby in 1876 to guide shipping on the river was demolished in 1954 and replaced by an automated light, which is now obsolete. LaHave's early history is commemorated by a cairn erected by the Historic Sites and Monuments Board and by the community's museum that was established in the former lightkeeper's dwelling.

Riverport, on the opposite shore, has a large sheltered harbour that was used by French supply vessels in the 1630s. It was once known as Anse-aux-huitres, or Oyster Cove, but later took the name Ritceys Cove from the Ritcey (formerly Henerici) family, who were prominent eighteenth-century settlers. It soon became an important fishing port. As the population grew, a change of name seemed desirable, and in the early twentieth century, the residents chose Riverport.

Shipbuilding, fishing, and fish processing were the main occupations in the nineteenth and early twentieth centuries. At the peak of the cod fishery, twenty-eight schooners sailed from its harbour, mostly going to Labrador and the offshore banks.

In the days of Prohibition, rum-running was a valuable sideline for many of the area's seamen, and Riverport's residents were deeply involved. Al Capone is said to have stayed at a hotel there while organizing shipments to the US. The local man behind much of this illegal trade was Willoughby Ritcey, who no longer went to sea because of an injury that had left him with a wooden leg. He financed the more active participants, many of whom were also members of the Ritcey clan. Rum-running was a risky business but very tempting for anyone with a boat looking to augment their income.

For many years, a passenger steamship service ran from Riverport to Bridgewater, operated by the LaHave Steamship Company, which also offered towing and freight services. The *Trusty* criss-crossed the river, picking up and dropping passengers at communities along the shore, while the tugboat *Samson* towed large sailing vessels into port.

At one time, Riverport had two churches, a hotel, a school, stores, a customs office, and post office. Ritcey Bros. Ltd. was a major employer in the area, with over six hundred workers in the fish plant, store, and other operations. A fire in 1920 destroyed the store along with other buildings and wharves. Reconstruction began almost immediately, and business continued, but another major fire in 1982, together with the decline in the cod stocks, devastated the Riverport fishery. Since then most of the small businesses have closed. Fishing continues, with a packing plant at Kraut Point, and shipbuilding is maintained on a smaller scale, in particular at the Covey Island Boat Works which built a major section of *Bluenose II*, as well as parts for the American schooner *Columbia*. They are best known for custom-built yachts and repairs.

Bridgewater takes its name from the first bridge over the LaHave River, built at the head of tide in the mid-1820s. A great deal of rum is reputed to have been consumed during its construction. Starratt's Hotel stood at the western edge of the bridge, and merchants set up businesses on the main street. With the Davison Lumber Company's sawmill just upriver, Bridgewater quickly grew into a busy port where many ships were built, and a lively lumber export trade developed. By the 1870s the main street was lined with stores, and the river was lined with wharves.

The LaHave River was becoming a busy highway by this time. The *Trusty* brought passengers to town from settlements downstream, large wooden ships left Bridgewater for distant ports, coastal vessels carried goods and passengers to and from ports in eastern Canada and the United States, and a regular passenger service ran between Bridgewater and Halifax.

A major fire in 1899 destroyed many of the town's buildings, but rebuilding quickly took place. Schooners and barques brought coal and other commodities for local merchants and exported lumber and pulp from mills on the river. The railway came to Bridgewater in 1889, and in the early 1900s the town became a railway junction, with lines going out to various communities.

Increasing competition from the railway and the construction of better roads brought changes to the town and to the river. Today, commercial shipping has given way to pleasure craft. Sawmills have closed, shipyards are quiet, and the big fishing schooners have long gone, as has the railway. For some time, the occasional barge laden with pulpwood could still be seen making its way down the river, but in recent years only private boats and some abandoned hulks are moored at Bridgewater's remaining wharf. It remains an important hub in the region, with a hospital and industrial park, and its heritage buildings are reminders of its prosperous mercantile past.

LaHave Islands

These islands, with their many sheltered harbours, are grouped together at the mouth of the river. Their colonial history dates back to the end of the eighteenth century when Henry Ferguson was granted an island to establish a fishery. It was originally known as Ferguson's Island and is now Moshers Island. The largest, Cape LaHave Island, was granted to a group of trustees for use by the people on both sides of the river as a common for pasturing their cattle. Farmers came every year on a day determined by the trustees to mow the marsh grass for hay, while their wives and children gathered cranberries. Today, kayakers enjoy visiting its beaches.

West Ironbound lies to the east of the entrance and is identified on early French maps as Île Marotte, named for Captain Bernard Marot, a man of many parts. A surgeon and ship's captain, he had been in Acadie in various capacities since about 1610, employed in the fishery and the fur trade, before serving Isaac de Razilly in the 1630s. The island served as a landmark for ships entering the harbour, and navigators were reminded to keep it on the starboard side of the ship.

West Ironbound was once home to a few fishing families, and to the keepers of the lighthouse that was constructed on the island in 1855. Despite this, the SS *Mount Temple* ran aground there in a storm in December 1907, carrying cargo and over six hundred passengers. The Wolfe family, who kept the light, were alerted by the urgent barking of their dog, Bosco, but the rescue could not begin until the storm died down the following day. Then the islanders used a line and a breeches buoy to bring the passengers and crew safely ashore. They were transported on the *Trusty* to Bridgewater, from where they travelled to Halifax. The *Mount Temple* was subsequently refloated.

Communities grew up at many of the other island harbours. By the late 1800s there were sixty-one families on the LaHave Islands making a living from fishing and keeping livestock, and visiting each other and the mainland by boat. Their locally built Bush Island boats were engaged in a productive inshore fishery, although men from the islands also worked as crewmen on the schooners out of Riverport.

WESTWARD TO SHELBURNE

The road continues along the coast, past many long inlets where Mi'kmaw encampments had existed for at least ten thousand years before European fishing vessels sheltered there. Later, Acadians, New England Planters, Loyalists, and others built homes and communities. The main road runs across the heads of these harbours, linking towns and villages along the coast.

Liverpool Bay and Harbour

The twisted estuary of the Mersey River forms a harbour at the head of Liverpool Bay. Champlain's map of the bay shows Mi'kmaw encampments both on the mainland and on the island at its entrance. The Mersey was a major route from Kejimkujik to the harbour called Ogomkigeak (dry sandy place) or Ogukegeok (place of departure).

In May 1604, Dugua de Mons's expedition anchored in the bay. They found not only the Mi'kmaq, but also a French vessel whose captain, Rossignol, was engaged in trading. As de Mons' company had been granted the monopoly of the fur trade in Acadie, Rossignol was arrested for illegal activities and his ship was seized. To commemorate this event, the French named the harbour Port Rossignol, and later the same name was given to a lake farther inland. According to Mi'kmaw lore, two of Rossignol's crew escaped up the river and settled at Kejimkujik.

In the early 1630s, Nicolas Denys established the first of his fishing stations on Herring Cove, at what is now Brooklyn. Unfortunately, while his ship was unloading in Portugal, war broke out between France and Spain. The ship and its cargo of fish were seized and his brother Simon imprisoned. Consequently, the enterprise in Nova Scotia failed and the harbour was abandoned. Twenty years later, when the British controlled Nova Scotia for a few years, Thomas Temple set up a temporary trading post there. After the territory was returned to France, a few Acadians settled at Port Rossignol. They continued to trade with the Mi'kmaq, who attacked and seized some New England fishing vessels in the ongoing struggle for control of the region.

In 1759, John Doggett and over fifty settlers from Massachusetts—called New England Planters—received grants in this township, with a town plan laid out around the harbour. It was originally called Lingley, in honour of an English admiral, but the name was soon changed to Liverpool. A small blockhouse, Fort Morris, was constructed for its defence.

The leaders of the early settlers were Doggett, Sylvanus Cobb, Elisha Freeman, and Simeon Perkins. We know a good deal about life in Liverpool during the latter part of the eighteenth century from Perkins's diary in which he recorded details of his own activities and those of the townsfolk. The house that he built for himself and his family is still standing.

From the start, the settlers made their living from the forest and the sea. The four leaders built sawmills and cut lumber from the surrounding forests. In 1765, Perkins had two schooners built, the first of many trading vessels of which he would have full or part ownership. Those who lived by fishing established themselves around the harbour and river mouth. The rocky ground and poor soil made it difficult to farm and grow food, so the settlers depended on ships bringing provisions into the harbour. Winters were particularly hard if supplies did not arrive, and on Christmas Day, 1773, Perkins wrote, "I work in the woods. No fresh provisions, so I dine on salt fish."

Lumbering, shipbuilding, and fishing continued to be the mainstays of the economy for the rest of the century and into the next. There was a ready market for lumber that was exported in locally built vessels. The harbour was busy as boats

Simeon Perkins built this house in Liverpool for his family.

from Liverpool sailed to the Grand Banks and Labrador, and trading ships carried dried salt cod to Europe and the West Indies.

The town was on the way to becoming prosperous when the American Revolution interrupted this progress. Some Liverpool residents left to join the rebels, and those who remained were torn between sympathy with their former compatriots and loyalty the British Crown. Nevertheless, the townsfolk had little choice but to defend themselves when privateers seized ships out of Liverpool and made off with their cargoes.

In 1778, a French ship pursued by a Royal Navy vessel ran aground in the harbour, and the two ships exchanged fire in a battle in which some of the French crew died and others were taken prisoner. American privateers made forays into the harbour to loot the wreck, and raided Liverpool itself before attempting to tow away the grounded vessel.

Simeon Perkins called out the militia and exchanged fire with the privateers for some time. After they left, a guard was set, but the raids continued. Perkins installed a battery on the waterfront, prepared Fort Morris to defend the town, and sent to Halifax for reinforcements. A company of the King's Orange Rangers arrived in the harbour in December. A further raid took place in 1780, when attackers landed after dark in a nearby cove and seized the fort and most of the Rangers. Perkins and his militia came to their rescue, captured one of the leading attackers, and negotiated for the release of the prisoners.

Meanwhile, in retaliation for their losses, Perkins and other Liverpool merchants obtained letters of marque permitting them to undertake privateering on their own account. Their first privateering vessel was the *Lucy*, bought in 1779, followed by several other vessels in which Perkins held shares. American ships and seized goods were valued by the Court of Admiralty, and prize money was awarded to the privateers' owners, bringing in a significant income for Liverpool merchants.

After the Revolution, Liverpool resumed its development, with the addition of some Loyalist settlers. Harbour trade flourished; merchants and ships' captains, shipbuilders and mill-owners became prosperous and built fine houses in the town.

Although the war was over, privateering was sufficiently lucrative that it resumed as other conflicts erupted. The most famous of the Liverpool privateering vessels was the *Rover*, built in Ichabod Darrow's shipyard on the north side of the harbour at what is now Brooklyn. She was commissioned in 1799 and had a short but significant career as a privateer in the war between Britain and Spain. Her captain, Alexander Godfrey, engaged the Spanish naval schooner *Santa Rita* and three gunships. Despite being outnumbered, men from the *Rover* seized the *Santa Rita* and sailed her back with seventy-one prisoners, and Godfrey became a local hero.

Privateering resumed in the War of 1812, and once again Liverpool merchants profited by the prize money they received. Only when international treaties outlawed the practice did privateers cease to operate from Liverpool Harbour.

In 1813, Liverpool experienced a tsunami. A huge wave came into the harbour, sweeping vessels from their moorings and tearing away the pilings of the wharves. Five ships were carried up the river, and as the water retreated, two others were washed over the bar and out to sea. It was generally concluded that this was the result of an undersea earthquake.

Towards the end of the century, the industrial prosperity that helped build the town's population and business wealth began its long decline. Shipyards and mills closed and the local bank failed, causing financial problems for many business owners. As the early twentieth century progressed, fishing vessels still left the harbour for the banks, but the introduction of refrigeration required that the traditional fishery adapt or perish.

Here, as elsewhere, a temporary bonus for adventurous boat owners came in the 1920s when Prohibition brought some wealth to the community, but in 1933, when the sale of alcohol in the United States was made legal, the rum-runners returned to their fishing and other business. Meanwhile, a pulp mill opened in 1929 at Brooklyn, across the harbour from Liverpool. For many years this landmark on the harbour was the area's chief employer. The mill lasted until the demand for pulp and paper rapidly waned, and after many years of poor sales, it closed in 2012. More recently, the site has been reactivated to grow and process marijuana, replacing some of the jobs that were lost.

Today, many Liverpool business owners focus on tourism, especially the annual Privateer Days celebration. Simeon Perkins's house has become a museum where visitors can observe the daily lives of his pioneer family. The adjacent Queens County Museum preserves relics from the town's past. The lighthouse at Fort Point, one of the oldest surviving lighthouses in the province, was decommissioned in 1989, but has been maintained as a small museum. The point has become a park from which visitors can look out to sea and imagine the busy harbour in the days of sail.

Coffin Island

Coffin Island at the harbour entrance, for many years the site of a Mi'kmaw encampment, was once known as Bear Island. It takes its name from one of the early settlers, Peleg Coffin, who came to the island from Nantucket as early as 1759 and received a large grant in 1764. Coffin and his fellow grantees developed a small fishing station on the island.

The original lighthouse at the south end of Coffin Island was among the earliest in the province. The cornerstone was laid by Simeon Perkins in 1811, and the building was completed the following year. It guided vessels safely into Liverpool Bay for a century before it was struck by lightning and burned down in 1913. It was replaced first by a concrete structure, then by a fibreglass building in a more protected location. There is no longer a lightkeeper on Coffin Island, but the automated light still guides vessels safely into Liverpool Bay.

Port Mouton

Farther along the coast, Pierre Dugua de Mons and his companions had resumed their explorations in May 1604 and were busy unloading their ship, *Don de Dieu*, in a new harbour, when a sheep fell overboard. *Splash!* This incident resulted in their naming the harbour Port-au-mouton—now Port Mouton, pronounced "Port Matoon."

The Mi'kmaq could find, in this area, all that they needed for their livelihood, including moose, rabbits, and game birds, as well as fish and shellfish in the harbour. The French set up a temporary camp, living off the land and building cabins, staying for about a month. They were awaiting word of a second vessel that had left France with them, carrying important supplies. The *Don de Dieu* had come farther south than originally planned, so de Mons sent the vessel that he had captured from Captain Rossignol to let the sister ship know where they were, while Champlain set off in a smaller vessel to explore the coast. After they had established contact with their supply ship, and Champlain had returned, they were ready to move on.

Two years later another French ship came into the harbour, bringing Jean de Poutrincourt and some new recruits to the settlement that de Mons's party had established at Port Royal. According to Marc Lescarbot, a French lawyer who later wrote an account of his travels, the ship had stopped to replenish supplies of wood and water, and the travellers "found the cabins and lodgings, yet whole and unbroken, that Monsieur de Monts [sic] made two years before." They also noticed the abundance of rabbits, and gathered some wild peas. But they stayed only briefly, leaving Port Mouton once more to the Mi'kmaq and to seasonal fishing vessels.

Nicolas Denys, in his account of Acadie, recalled that when he was in the area in the 1630s he had seen "ships there making the cod fishery; they go about two and a half leagues to find the Cod, which they dry upon flakes; these are a kind of hurdles, on which one is obliged to dry the fish when there occur at the place of the fishery only sand or grass." This practice of drying fish on flakes continued along Nova Scotia's coasts until well into the twentieth century.

When Denys's great-nephew, Simon Denys de Bonnaventure, stopped at Port Mouton in 1701, there were fishing stations on the main island in the harbour, and on two of the smaller islands. But any Acadians still there in 1756 were exiled, and after that, fishing vessels in the harbour were just as likely to be based in New England as on the shore.

About two decades later Deputy Surveyor William Morris was sent to lay out a settlement at the head of Port Mouton harbour to accommodate Loyalist refugees. It was to be named Guysborough, in honour of Sir Guy Carleton, and like other Loyalist towns, the streets were laid out in an orderly grid pattern. That was about the only thing that was orderly in the settlement. On October 17, 1783, a ship came into harbour carrying three hundred people, soldiers of Tarleton's Legion who had fought in the war, with their families. Shortly afterwards they were joined by a contingent of Black Loyalists, followed by over two thousand more people, many of whom had formerly held office jobs at the British commissary in New York.

Guysborough's troubles began immediately. Because the settlement had been thrown together so hastily, there was an inadequate quantity of rations and building supplies, and many people lacked both food and materials for their houses. There were several deaths, and the suffering was made worse when supplies were delayed. The final indignity was that no provision had been made for a burial ground, so a makeshift graveyard was hastily created. Disputes soon broke out between the men who had fought in the war and those who had spent their time behind desks.

Having endured a miserable winter rife with dissention, and realizing that there was no way they could make a living from the barren, rocky soil, many decided to leave. Their departure was hastened by a disastrous fire that destroyed the town's recently erected buildings. In May 1784, ships left for New Brunswick, and for Chedabucto Bay where they founded a new Guysborough.

Those who remained established the present village of Port Mouton. Many took up fishing and boat building and prospered until the decline of the fishery in the twentieth century. Today, the population has dwindled, the local school has closed, and children now attend school in Liverpool. But Port Mouton is still a fishing village, with two operating fish plants and a fish farm in the bay, which has aroused opposition from local fishers who claim that it has harmed the lobster stocks.

In summer, tourists enjoy the local beaches. The spot where Champlain set foot over four centuries ago is now part of Kejimkujik National Park Seaside.

Shelburne Harbour

The road from Port Mouton passes several long inlets from the Atlantic before reaching the head of Shelburne Harbour. Many people who have never visited the town of Shelburne have seen its historic buildings in movies. They formed the backdrop for the 1995 production of *The Scarlet Letter*, and more recently, for the 2015 television miniseries *The Book of Negroes*. Walking through narrow streets between restored buildings is like stepping into the late eighteenth century.

Although Shelburne is considered to have the world's third-best natural harbour, it has never achieved the commercial potential that this advantage suggests. Before the colonial period, the Mi'kmaq called the harbour Logumkeegan—sometimes written Sogumkeagum—and the French called it Port Razoir. Initially, the English called it Port Roseway (the English form of Razoir) and the river that flows through the town is still the Roseway.

There was a fluctuating Acadian population at the end of the seventeenth century, but few details have survived about the inhabitants. In 1699, Joseph Robineau de Villebon was reporting to Louis XIV about conditions in Acadie. He described

Port Razoir as follows: "One of the finest harbours on the coast. Its entrance is suitable for all vessels, and there is abundant fishing. The soil is suitable for cultivation, and there are many red oaks. Another of Sr. d'Entremont's sons lives here with his wife and four children, ten or twelve horned cattle, and some sheep. There is another settler with a wife and two children. He is not prosperous but is a capable fisherman."

Constant raids from New Englanders forced the few people who were still living on the harbour in the early eighteenth century to abandon the settlement, but the raiders were equally insecure. In 1715, Captain Cyprian Southack tried to establish a fishing base, but it was attacked and burned down by the Mi'kmaq. New England fishing vessels continued to shelter in the harbour but there was no settlement on the shore. In 1723, pirate Ned Low captured thirteen of their ships and took one man prisoner.

In the 1760s, Alexander McNutt received a grant to form a settlement on the harbour, to be named New Jerusalem, but like his other grandiose schemes, it failed. The only place where he succeeded in establishing a handful of settlers was on the island in the mouth of the harbour.

The American Revolution brought thousands of Loyalists to Nova Scotia. Port Roseway's impressive harbour made it a potentially ideal location for people interested in fishing and trading. About fifteen hundred refugees who had gathered in New York in 1782 formed the Port Roseway Associates, and provision was made for them to come to what would become known as Shelburne, on the east side of the harbour. These first Loyalists arrived in May 1783, and soon their numbers had risen to five thousand. Ships continued to bring would-be settlers into the harbour, and by the following year the population of the new town amounted to over ten thousand. Deputy Surveyor Benjamin Marston was frantically surveying new lots to accommodate them. It was gruelling work, the terrain was rocky and unpromising, and Marston complained bitterly about the heat and the mosquitoes.

For the first few years, the government supplied provisions while homes were built and businesses established. But many of the newcomers were townspeople who could not cope with the rough living and hard work needed to build a new settlement. Either they returned to the United States or went elsewhere in the colony. Those who remained found that fishing, shipbuilding, and merchant shipping would sustain them and the community. They organized a fire brigade to protect their town's wooden buildings, many of which can be seen today, in real life or in the movies.

In fact, within about twenty years, most of the thousands of people who had sailed into the harbour in the 1780s hoping to get a new start had sailed back out

By the early twentieth century Shelburne had become a busy fishing port.

again, and many of the houses built by the Loyalists were empty and falling into disrepair. There were two Scottish merchants, however, George and Robert Ross, who opened a general store in Shelburne in 1787 and operated a trading business, bringing in stock from the West Indies, the United States, and even Europe. In 1815, they sold the store to Robert Thomson, whose son continued to run it until 1880. The Ross-Thomson house and store are still standing, and the public can experience Shelburne's past at this museum—part of the Nova Scotia Museum complex.

There were difficult times in the fishery, which had an impact on the economy, as Lord Dalhousie, lieutenant-governor of Nova Scotia, discovered when he arrived in the harbour on HMS *Leander* in July 1817. He reported, "Shelburne is the picture of despair and wretchedness. The population does not exceed 90 families, perhaps in all 400 people. The large homes, rotten & tumbling into the once fine & broad streets, the inhabitants crawling about idle and careworn in appearance, sunk in poverty and dejected in spirits."

The harbour was protected by "a miserable decayed battery close to the town, six guns mounted and one Artilleryman in charge." Across the harbour on the western side, the militia barracks were "falling into utter ruin" and deemed "too far from the town to be of any use." This was a low point in Shelburne's history.

By the 1820s, the population was only about three hundred strong. Another visitor described seeing "a few large structures, with decaying timbers and broken window frames, standing by the wharfs which must have once teemed with ship masters and sailors." Nevertheless, the residents of Shelburne recovered as the century progressed. Sawmills were built on the river and shipyards were busy. Fishing schooners left for the banks and returned with cargoes of cod to be processed for export. Merchant ships brought back goods from around the world, and Shelburne Harbour became a busy place.

The twentieth century brought change, as shipyards closed and the fishery declined. But the town survived, and today, Shelburne Harbour has a shipyard and a dory shop and a fishery, as well as many tourist attractions and services.

Birchtown

Among the Loyalists who came to Port Roseway were about five hundred Free Blacks, including many former slaves who had earned their liberty by fighting for the British. They were given land on the far side of the harbour, in the settlement of Birchtown. The population soon swelled to twenty-five hundred, but they found the land inhospitable, the people of Shelburne unwelcoming, and the government slow to provide them with farm lots where they might grow their own provisions and keep cows, pigs, and chickens. They were prepared to work for low wages in Shelburne but clashed violently with some of the white settlers who were competing for jobs.

Most Birchtown residents lived in poverty, and when the chance came to emigrate to Sierra Leone in 1792, many of them seized it. Those who remained formed a resilient community, building a school and a church by the nineteenth century, but the opportunities for employment lay elsewhere, and only about two hundred now live in the area.

The Black Loyalist Heritage Museum opened at Birchtown's original site in 2015, telling the story of slavery and the hardships endured by the early Black settlers. Their names were recorded in 1782 in the "Book of Negroes," a register of those who embarked in New York for Nova Scotia. This document became the basis for Lawrence Hill's book and the television miniseries of the same name, filmed in and around Shelburne and Birchtown.

McNutts Island

The island at the entrance to Shelburne Harbour that the Acadians called Île Razoir once provided a summer fishing base for the Indigenous inhabitants of the region. Its later history begins in the early 1760s, when Alexander McNutt and his brother Benjamin received a grant on the island, where they attempted to settle thirty-seven of the Port Roseway Associates. The island's rocky soil was generally unsuitable for agriculture, but the McNutts chose the best acreage, including a small harbour, where they established a farm. Only a few of the new settlers stayed on their inhospitable lots. Alexander himself was rarely on the island, siding with the rebels during the American Revolution and leaving his brother to manage the farm. He returned to the island at the end of the war, but in 1796 he left for Virginia, where he spent the rest of his life.

The first lighthouse to guide shipping into Shelburne Harbour, and the third to be established in the province, was built in 1788 on Cape Roseway, at the southern tip of the island. It operated until it was struck by lightning and burned in 1959. The first lightkeeper, Alexander Cocken or Cockeron, served until his death in 1812, when he was succeeded by his son, who ran a boys' school at the light station. The last lightkeeper retired in 1986, when the light was automated.

Descendants of the few settlers who remained on the island continued to live there into the early twentieth century. They managed to cultivate small subsistence farms, made their livings from the sea, and at least one boat, the *Laconic*, was built there in 1880.

The island was recognized as strategically important and was one of the sites where the French considered building a fort in the seventeenth century. During the Second World War it was fortified and occupied by soldiers, in case the enemy attempted to land. When the war ended, a German U-boat surrendered to the Canadian Navy in Shelburne Harbour.

Today, tourists who visit the island can enjoy a hike on the trail to the lighthouse, and visit New Jerusalem Farm, the historic site first settled by the McNutt brothers.

CAPE SABLE AREA

The road continues from Shelburne through the area that the Mi'kmaq know as Kesputwik—the Land Ends. Basque sailors engaged in the fishery gave Baccaro Point its name from their word for cod, *baccalaos*. The French name Cap-de-sable referred to the sandy beaches and was applied to the area as a whole, as well as to the cape and the island.

Port LaTour

The grassy outline of an old fort can be seen clearly on the western side of Port LaTour Harbour. It is a vestige of a small community of fur traders led by Charles de LaTour, who first came to Acadie as a young man in 1606 to join the settlers at the Port Royal Habitation. However, after it was abandoned, he and his cousin Charles de Biencourt spent some years on the move with about twenty French followers, befriending and sharing the lifestyle of the Mi'kmaq, and sending furs back for sale in France. After Biencourt died in 1623, the leadership passed to LaTour.

In the late 1620s, LaTour established a fur-trading post and built Fort St. Louis on the harbour, near Baccaro Point. Opinions have differed over the years as to the exact location of this fort, but archaeologists believe it stood on the east side of the peninsula at today's Port LaTour, where the outline is visible. Artifacts recovered during excavations support this.

These were turbulent times in Acadie: LaTour was frequently threatened with attack by his rival, Charles de Menou d'Aulnay, and the British were laying claim to what they called Nova Scotia, or New Scotland. LaTour desperately needed supplies from France. His father Claude came to Acadie in 1630 with a British expedition to a fort they had established on the Annapolis Basin. He had accepted two of the newly created Scottish baronetcies of Nova Scotia on behalf of himself and Charles. Confident that he had found a solution to his son's problems by going over to the British, he was dismayed when Charles refused the deal, affirming his loyalty to the King of France. After a two-day battle in the harbour, Claude was forced to sail away with the British expedition.

Fortunately for Charles, two French ships soon arrived with food, supplies, and three Récollet fathers. LaTour's union with his Indigenous wife received the church's blessing, and their daughters were baptized. In 1631, LaTour finally received a long-awaited commission from King Louis giving him full authority in Acadie.

After the death of his first wife, LaTour was left without a son to inherit his property and decided to remarry. He sent an agent to France with the mission of finding him a wife, and in 1640, his ship sailed into the harbour with his bride-to-be, Françoise-Marie Jacquelin. Not long afterwards, LaTour was forced to cede Fort Saint-Louis to Charles de Menou d'Aulnay, who also claimed authority in Acadie. He retreated to his fort on the St. John River, where his second wife died tragically, after attempting to defend it against d'Aulnay's raiders. After his enemy's death, LaTour was married a third time, to d'Aulnay's widow, and returned with her to Port LaTour, where he died in 1666.

For a few years in the mid-seventeenth century when Nova Scotia was under British rule, Port LaTour was refortified by Thomas Temple, but Acadie was returned to France in 1667. After the Expulsion, New Englanders replaced the Acadian residents and established a fishery at Port LaTour. Fishing boats still use the harbour, and seafood is processed and exported from Upper Port LaTour.

Barrington Bay

Barrington's built heritage—the Old Meeting House, Woolen Mill, and nearby Old Court House—recall the history of a community founded by Planters in the 1760s. But the history of the area goes further back, to the days when the Mi'kmaq lived in wigwams close to the shore at a place at the head of the bay that they called Ministugek.

During the seventeenth and early eighteenth centuries, a small Acadian population grew up around the bay to the west of Baccaro Point. The residents lived peacefully, farming and fishing, until April 1756 when English troops were rounding up any Acadians who had not been deported the previous year. They surprised the residents in their beds and loaded them on a transport ship to carry them into exile.

Just four years later, Barrington Township, comprising the area between Negro Harbour and the Yarmouth county line, was established for New England Planters. Barrington town was laid out on a little harbour near the head of bay, now known as Barrington Head. Twelve families from the Cape Cod area were the first to take up the offer of land. They found the remains of Acadian homes and abandoned fields, and made a living from fishing and lumbering. Shipbuilding began with the construction of the *Sally*, owned by William Greenwood, and trading vessels brought in goods in exchange for fish.

In about 1771 they began to build the Old Meeting House, where both public meetings and religious services were held. After a while it was determined that it should serve only religious purposes, and civic meetings were conducted in private homes or in a schoolhouse until the Old Court House was built in 1843 to administer the affairs of the township and serve as a town hall and jail. The Old Meeting House is open to the public in summer as part of the Nova Scotia Museum.

The American Revolution brought privateers to the harbour, seizing ships and raiding homes on the shore. In its aftermath some Loyalists arrived from overcrowded Shelburne and by the end of the century there were 127 families in

Barrington Township, including ten families in Barrington Passage who were freed slaves.

Fishing villages were scattered from Cape Negro to Shag Harbour, and on the islands in the bay. Fishing was a lucrative occupation during the nineteenth and early twentieth centuries, and the opening of lobster canneries in the township brought employment and prosperity. A fleet of about sixty-five merchant vessels, some locally built, had Barrington Bay as their home port.

In addition to this busy port and fishery, from 1882 until 1962, the Barrington Woolen Mill processed and exported wool from local sheep. Today it operates as part of the Nova Scotia Museum and attracts visitors to the area.

The ocean always has its dangers and this area saw its share of shipwrecks. In 1850, a dramatic rescue took place when Captain William Henry Coffin set out from Barrington in a hurricane to rescue the crew of the brigantine *Eliza Helen*, and was able to bring them safely to shore. Shortly after that incident, a lighthouse was built on Baccaro Point to safeguard shipping. It began operation in 1851, and was supplemented in 1875 by a lightship, the *Barrington*, moored off the dangerous Brant Ledges. The lightship came adrift in a storm in 1919 and ended up in Barrington Harbour, where the lightkeeper was able to walk ashore.

Before modern highways were built, a regular shipping service was provided to this area by the steamer *Latour* that carried passengers and freight between Yarmouth and Lockeport, calling at Barrington Passage and other ports.

The last schooner built at Barrington Passage was launched in 1967. Today, lobster is the main catch, and local businesses supply equipment for both commercial and recreational vessels. The town's historic buildings attract visitors, many of whom stop to enjoy a meal of lobster or other seafood in nearby restaurants.

Cape Sable Island

Cape Sable Island (not to be confused with the remote Sable Island) takes its name from the sandy cape off its southern tip. Today it is reached by a causeway, but early settlers travelled by sea. French fishing boats operated in its harbours, and during the seventeenth and early eighteenth centuries there were ongoing disputes between them and vessels from New England that fished in the nearby waters. After the Expulsion, any Acadians who still lived on the island were arrested and imprisoned. New Englanders who accepted the government's offer of land there in the 1760s were already familiar with the fishing grounds. They included Quakers from Cape Cod and Nantucket who planned to set up a whaling station, but in the end few of them remained on the island.

Cape Island fishing boats in harbour, 1949.

Although most of the settlers were occupied with fishing, the one whose name is remembered today in a small community museum was a tanner and a shoemaker: Archelaus Smith and his wife, Elizabeth, came from Barrington, where they had lived for about thirteen years before moving to the island and settling at Centreville, on McGrays Cove. Smith became a community leader, probably providing footwear for the local men and women, as well as acting as clerk to the proprietors, magistrate, and surveyor. The Archelaus Smith Museum preserves the history of the island's residents.

Shipwrecks were common on the dangerous ledges off Cape Sable Island. Seal Island Lighthouse was built in 1830, but it did not prevent the American packet ship *Staffordshire* from striking Blonde Rock in 1853, with the loss of 170 lives. After another particularly disastrous wreck in 1860, when two hundred lives were lost from the steamship *Hungarian*, another lighthouse was installed at Cape Sable, on an island to the south of the main island. A Marconi wireless station was established nearby that remained in operation until the First World War, when it served as a naval wireless finding station until 1920. The light was automated in the late 1980s, and the cape is now home only to a flock of sheep.

Another lighthouse was built in the early 1870s on Bon Portage Island, off Clarks Harbour. Its best-known keeper was Morrill Richardson, who came to the island in 1929 and maintained the light for thirty-five years. This lightkeeper and his family became the subject of a very popular memoir titled *We Keep a Light*, written by his wife, Evelyn Richardson, which would go on to win a Governor General's Award. The old wooden tower with its adjoining family home was replaced by a concrete structure in 1964. It has since been automated and continues to guide vessels entering harbour.

Clarks Harbour became the centre of the island's fishery, which was a major export industry by the beginning of the twentieth century. Four of the island's six lobster canneries, as well as other fish processing plants, were at Clarks Harbour, and its boatyards were busy. With the decline of the age of sail, a new kind of fishing boat, the Cape Islander, was built in Ephraim Anderson's boatyard. These motorized wooden vessels quickly became popular with the inshore fishery throughout the Atlantic region. Several boat builders now operate in Clarks Harbour. After over a century, Cape Island boats are still the main lobster fishing vessels around our coasts. Many today are made of fibreglass instead of wood.

A new industry came to Clarks Harbour around 1940, to satisfy a market for kelp that could be harvested among the ledges offshore and around nearby islands. A plant on the wharf packed the product for shipping to the United States. This business lasted for several years until the demand for kelp dried up.

While several varieties of fish are caught year-round, the focus today is the lucrative lobster fishery. "Dumping Day" at the end of November, when the first lobster traps are taken out to sea and dropped at chosen locations, is eagerly awaited. For the next few months, until the end of May, boats bring the valuable catch to shore to be packed for export. Lobster fishing has brought prosperity to the island, now known as the lobster capital of Canada.

Shag Harbour

What in the world was that? Most people had never heard of Shag Harbour until an extraordinary event in 1967 hit the headlines and captured public attention. A strange object had appeared in the sky and dropped into the waters of the harbour, but the mystery of what it was has never really been solved.

Shag Harbour lies at the western edge of what was originally Barrington Township, now the Municipality of Barrington. As the population of the township increased, people in search of land spread westward. The Nickerson and Kendrick families were among the first to move to Shag Harbour, where Joshua Nickerson established a shipyard. Fishing has always been an important part of the economy, and boat building was carried on around the harbour for many years. The Halliday family's boat shop was at Bear Point, and Andrew Larkin and Elroy Shand began a small dory business in the 1930s which produced nearly two hundred boats before it closed in 1972.

In the 1940s Shag Harbour was found to be an important source of Irish moss or carrageen moss—a red seaweed found along the coast. A moss-drying plant operated for several years in the village, exporting bales to the United States, until competition drove them out of business.

The most eventful moment in Shag Harbour's history came when residents saw mysterious lights in the sky, and what appeared to be a round object crashing into the water off the harbour. There it floated for a time, leaving a trail of yellow foam, before sinking. Thinking that it might have been a plane, local boat-owners and the RCMP set out to search for survivors, but nothing was found and no planes were reported missing. After much speculation, it was eventually classified as an Unidentified Flying Object (UFO), but the mystery remains. In 2019, the Canadian mint issued a glow-in-the-dark coin that commemorated the eerie event.

Acadian Shore

This journey to southwestern Nova Scotia continues with an exploration of the long, deep harbours that run from Pubnico to Yarmouth, until the scenery changes to the smoother coastline of St. Marys Bay.

This region, particularly the area in Digby County known as the District of Clare, is home to many Acadians, descendants of the families that were deported from Nova Scotia between 1755 and 1757. When they made their way back in the 1760s, they found that their farms had been taken over by New Englanders, and instead, they were given land in this southwestern region. Only the people of Pobomcoup—renamed Pubnico by the English—returned to their familiar harbour.

Before the Expulsion, most Acadians had farmed fertile dykelands around the Bay of Fundy. The area where they found themselves on their return was less suitable for farming, but there were forests and rich fishing grounds, so they turned to forestry, shipbuilding, and fishing.

Not all communities on the Acadian Shore are predominantly French speaking. Land was also granted to New Englanders, and the place names are a mixture of French and English.

PUBNICO HARBOUR

The coast road winds around to the eastern shore of Pubnico Harbour, where there are English- and French-speaking residents. On the western shore, however, there are predominantly francophones, many of whom have the family name of d'Entremont. In 1653, Charles de LaTour granted to his friend Philippe Mius d'Entremont a tract of land on the east side of the harbour that the Mi'kmaw called Pogomkook. D'Entremont was made baron of what the French referred to as Pobomcoup, where he settled with his wife, Madeleine Hélie, and their daughter, Marguerite.

The d'Entremonts went on to have four more children, three boys and another girl. They built a manor house on the hill overlooking the harbour, cleared land for farming, and established a water-powered mill. A chapel and a presbytery stood nearby. D'Entremont brought in farm labourers and other settlers, and a small community developed around his estate. He was appointed king's attorney, and in later life moved to Port Royal, leaving his land and his title to his eldest son, Jacques, who married LaTour's daughter Anne.

Jacques was running the estate when Governor Villebon visited Pobomcoup in 1699 and wrote of its progress: "The soil is fertile, and there is good fishing within sight of land. One of the sons of the Sr. d'Entremont lives there with his wife and eight children. …[I]n the spring, the peas and wheat were well up; he has 30 horned cattle, 3 sheep and 18 pigs; also a watermill."

The village continued to grow; most of Philippe's children remained in Pobomcoup, where they were joined by other families. By the middle of the eighteenth century there were about twenty households on the east side of the harbour, and a few houses on the west side.

The village was left undisturbed when the Expulsion began in 1755, but the following year, British ships sailed into the harbour and rounded up Acadian men, women, and children. The d'Entremonts were deported along with the other families to Massachusetts, where Jacques died. In 1758 English troops returned to search for any Acadians who had escaped the previous raid. Their leader, Joseph Gorham, described it as a "very large Village, where there is a Mass house, & several dwelling houses… there is potatoes &c. in the ground, I believe nigh three hundred bushels." Then the English burned the farms and houses to ensure that anyone who had escaped deportation did not return to the village.

When the survivors returned to Nova Scotia in 1766, they found that their former land on the upper east side of the harbour had been taken over by English settlers—the Larkins, Goodwins, and Seeleys. Land was still available towards the harbour mouth, where the Belliveau and Amirault families established themselves, while the d'Entremonts, including Jacques's grandson Benoni, settled on the west side. He became a community leader and a justice of the peace.

The population increased as the Duon (d'Éon), Surette, LeBlanc, and other families found their way to Pubnico. Homes grew up on both sides of the harbour and residents began to make their livings from the sea. Soon after returning from exile, Benoni d'Entremont built a ship, *Le Bonaventure*, which he used for fishing and coastal trading. On one occasion, he encountered American privateers who seized his vessel, but he and his men were able to fight them off and recapture the ship. Two more ships were built in Pubnico before the end of the eighteenth

In the 1950s, fish was dried on flakes along the shore at West Pubnico.

century, and the industry grew. During the second half of the nineteenth century Pubnico's shipyards produced as many as 130 vessels.

In September 1721, a strange boat appeared in the harbour carrying the survivors from the ship *Hannah* that had been wrecked among the Tusket Islands. Charles d'Entremont and Pierre Landry took them to their destination in Annapolis Royal in Charles's sloop *Beaufils*. Despite attempts to salvage some of the *Hannah*'s cargo, the goods had disappeared.

In April 1736, another apparent shipwreck survivor was brought into Pubnico Harbour. She said she was Susanna Buckler, the wife of the *Baltimore*'s owner; the ship had been blown off course into Chebogue Harbour where the Mi'kmaq had raided and looted her, and Captain Buckler and many of the crew had died. Susanna had supposedly been taken by the Mi'kmaq, among whom she was found by Charles d'Entremont, who brought her to Pubnico and then escorted her to Annapolis Royal. Subsequent enquiries revealed that her story was a complete fabrication. Susanna was in fact one of a group of convicts being deported from Dublin to Maryland who had mutinied, massacred the crew and seized the ship. The good people of Pubnico who had helped her were not too happy to have been so deceived.

Fishing, fish processing, and boat building continue to be the main employment for residents on both sides of the harbour, as they were in the nineteenth and twentieth centuries. In the past, there was always plenty of work for carpenters, shipwrights, and sailmakers, for ships' crews, and for workers who dried the salt cod on flakes along the shore. In the glory days of the cod fishery, larger schooners sailed for the Grand Banks, while smaller vessels fished closer to home. Outfitting them with provisions for the voyage made business for local merchants.

A lighthouse on the east side of the harbour guided ships safely into port. The first lightkeeper, Maturin Amiro, moved into the house provided for him, and as his family increased, he added to it over the years until it consisted of more than twenty rooms. A second lighthouse, built in 1889, with less commodious living quarters, was replaced by the present automated fibreglass tower.

The tourist season brings many visitors to the area, and the Acadian Museum and Archives at West Pubnico preserves artifacts illustrating the area's history. It also houses the vast collection of historical records assembled by Père Clarence d'Entremont, a descendant of the founder of the community. At Lower West Pubnico, the Historic Acadian Village recreates the former Acadian way of life in a group of nineteenth-century buildings, where animators in period costume demonstrate traditional skills and crafts. The residents of Pubnico are proud of their history and Acadian culture.

TOWNSHIP OF ARGYLE

The highway through the Municipality (formerly Township) of Argyle allows travellers to glimpse some of the many inlets and islands of Lobster Bay, between Pubnico and Tusket. The Township was created in 1759, extending around the entire bay, with its many small coves and harbours. In some places, Acadian flags are flying, and signage is a mixture of French and English. The French came here first in the mid-1600s, when Charles de LaTour established a trading post on what is now Roberts Island. Later, a few Acadian families from Port Royal found sufficient marshland on the river estuaries to continue their traditional style of farming. In the aftermath of the 1755 Expulsion, those who escaped deportation fled to the woods. In the 1760s, land was granted both to New Englanders and to returning

Acadian families, and many of their descendants have remained in the area. The administrative centre of Argyle Township was established at Tusket.

Tusket

Tusket is now a quiet fishing village at the head of the long harbour formed by the estuary of the Tusket River. Its most outstanding building is its former courthouse and jail, with its bell tower. Built in 1805, it is the oldest courthouse still standing in Canada. Tusket is a name that derives from Neketaousksit, meaning in Mi'kmaw "great forked tidal river." In this area, before displacement by colonial settlement, the Mi'kmaq harvested food from the sea and the land, where many species of fish, shellfish, waterfowl, and mammals were plentiful. The Acadians who came here called the area Tousquet. A few families built dykes, drained the riverside salt-marshes, and established farms before deportation. When they returned to Nova Scotia after 1763, the Amirault, Moulaison, Mius, and Doucette families were granted land on the river, south of today's village.

In 1784 and 1785, Loyalist refugees from New York and New Jersey, escaping from overcrowded Shelburne, also received grants in this part of Argyle Township. Most of them settled on the east side of the Tusket River, but one man, Jacob Tooker, chose to live on the west side. Being a master shipbuilder, he soon established the first of many shipyards that would grow up along the river.

The most prominent man in the newly established community on the east side of the river was James Lent—known as Squire Lent. He came from Tappan, New York, with his family and servants, and he built one of the first houses in Tusket. He set up a fishing business, exporting his catch to the West Indies and bringing rum, molasses, and other goods into port.

Sailors are often called upon to assist others in distress, and people from Tusket went to the rescue in 1801 when a boat carrying five survivors from the brig *Industry*, which had caught fire and sunk far away in the Bay of Fundy, fetched up on the nearby rocks. The boat had been adrift for a week, and most of the twenty-five people aboard had perished from cold and hunger. The locals rescued the captain and the crewmen who had made it to shore and transported them to Yarmouth.

The fishery prospered in the nineteenth century, when salmon, herring, and gaspereau were plentiful in the estuary. By mid-century, Tusket had grown to become an important shipbuilding centre. Many Acadians found work as labourers in the sawmills and shipyards which flourished over the next twenty years. Tusket shipyards became known for producing some of the largest vessels in the province,

Fishing sheds used for the gaspereau fishery at Tusket Falls, at the head of the harbour, were still standing in 1914 but have since disappeared.

and their launchings were great public events, but the town suffered the same fate as other shipbuilding communities at the end of the century.

The courthouse served its original purpose until 1944, and the following year it became the offices of the Municipality of Argyle. Today, it houses the area's museum.

The prosperity that Tusket had enjoyed in the age of sail diminished with the changing economy of the twentieth century, and the village fell on hard times. Today, there are fewer than four hundred permanent residents, and the majority are Acadians. With a variety of fish in the river, sport fishing has become an important attraction. Tusket is an educational centre for the region, and visitors can learn about the area's history from the well-organized resources of the Argyle Township Court House Museum and Archives.

Wedgeport

Wedgeport lies on the harbour of Goose Bay, at the western side of Tusket Wedge. Despite its English name, it was settled in the 1760s by returning Acadian families.

In 1769 they were visited by a priest, who said mass on a hill on which a cross was later erected. The hill is still known as Butte-de-la-Croix and is maintained by the community as a historic site.

The original settlers were soon joined by others, and the community began to grow. The brothers Sylvain and Charles-Amand Pothier took an important part in its development. They operated a successful fishing and shipping business, with eleven sailing ships and seventy smaller fishing boats based in the harbour. Many of the residents were employed on fishing boats, or in processing the cod and mackerel that were valuable exports.

Today Wedgeport has a prosperous lobster fishery and a long tradition of boat building. In addition, is also a base for sport tuna fishing and runs an annual Tuna Tournament and Festival.

CHEBOGUE HARBOUR

The village of Arcadia, lying just over the border into Yarmouth Municipality, lies on the banks of the Chebogue River that runs into Chebogue Harbour. Stone tools found in this area date back at least seven thousand years. Its name is derived from a Mi'kmaw name, Tkebok (spelled various ways), thought to mean "big marsh" or "big meadow." In the seventeenth century the French called it Teboc, but the name changed over the years to Chebogue. Chebogue Point at the harbour mouth is reputed to be the spot where David Lomeron, a merchant from La Rochelle, set up a fur-trading post sometime around 1614. A few years later, during the time when the British first laid claim to Nova Scotia and maintained a garrison at Port Royal, Lomeron's fort was raided and destroyed by the Scottish Kirke brothers.

A strange event took place at Chebogue Harbour in 1713, when an English brigantine, the *Baltimore*, anchored there, supposedly to take on fresh water. She was carrying sixty-six convicts who were being transported from Dublin to Maryland. They had organized a mutiny, massacred the crew and taken over the ship, and then vanished into the forest, with most of the ship's rigging and cargo. One woman was found there the following April and taken to Pubnico, where she deceived her rescuers by saying she was the ship-owner's wife.

In the 1740s, eight Acadian families came to Chebogue from Port Royal, finding suitable farmland on the marshes around the harbour. They built a chapel on the east side. However, they were not allowed to enjoy their new homes for long before being deported to France in 1756. Two years later British troops returned to complete the destruction of their homes, and they found on their return that their land had been granted to settlers from New England.

These settlers began to come to Chebogue in the 1760s, seizing the opportunity to revive the Acadian farmlands. In 1769, John Clements and his family sailed in from Massachusetts, bringing materials to rebuild their home. The Clements House—one of the oldest in the county—had been carefully taken down and loaded onto a ship to be reassembled in Chebogue, where it was occupied by the family for many years. John died in 1805, but several members of his family remained in Chebogue and are buried in the local cemetery.

Chebogue was for a time the most important community in the area. A few years after the settlers arrived, construction of the first church in Yarmouth County was begun and completed in 1773. Most people in Chebogue took up fishing or farming.

In 1777, during the American Revolution, a confrontation took place off Chebogue Harbour between three American privateers and the HMS *Milford*. One of the American vessels, the *Cabot*, became separated from the others and was chased into the harbour, where it ran aground. The crew escaped into the village, and several of them were taken in by a family sympathetic to the rebels, before eventually making their way home.

Farming, fishing, and merchant shipping provided a good living for Chebogue residents in the nineteenth century. Today, some descendants of the early settlers remain in the small community.

YARMOUTH

Yarmouth's Cape Forchu Lighthouse is a significant landmark on this tour of harbours. The cape and harbour were first described by Champlain, who was exploring the coast of Nova Scotia in 1604 in search of a suitable site for a settlement and trading post. He wrote, "We came to a cape that we named Fourchu … This harbour is good for vessels at its entrance, but at the head it is almost dry at low tide, except for a little river surrounded by meadows, which make it quite a pleasant place. Cod fishing is good near the harbour."

Champlain and his companions did not linger, and the next French visitor to the harbour was Nicolas Denys, who remarked on the abundance of cod not far from the shore. These seventeenth-century travellers say nothing of the Mi'kmaq who lived around the harbour and inland around the lakes. Examples of the stone tools used before contact with Europeans can be seen in the Yarmouth County

Museum, along with examples of Mi'kmaw crafts, including items decorated with porcupine quills in intricate designs, and leather clothing ornamented with traditional motifs, all demonstrating skilled artistry.

The nearby meadows and the availability of good fishing made an attractive location for the small community of Acadians who settled here before being deported. They were replaced in 1761 by the Landers, Ellis, and Perry families from Yarmouth, Massachusetts, who brought the name of their former home with them. They were joined in 1767 by some returning Acadian families.

As settlement in Yarmouth expanded, the Mi'kmaq retreated farther inland to lakes and forests, where they could maintain their traditional way of life, but lumbering, settlement, and road building continued to encroach on their communities. Today, some Mi'kmaq live in the Yarmouth First Nation Reserve established in 1887, one of the Acadia First Nations communities, while others live in the nearby communities.

In 1775, during the American Revolution, two American privateer vessels raided Yarmouth, seized the militia officers who tried to defend the town, and pillaged the community. Some of the settlers sympathized with their former neighbours, and would gladly have returned to New England, but were not permitted to do so.

At the end of the war, the population expanded quickly with the arrival of Loyalists, and Yarmouth became largely English-speaking. It was an important shipbuilding centre in the nineteenth century, and the harbour was busy with both commercial and fishing vessels. A visitor in the 1820s observed "two or three square-rigged vessels and sundry smaller craft lying in the harbour." By the late 1860s, Yarmouth was said to have more vessels per capita than any other port of similar size. It was close to major American ports, and its trading ships could be found all over the world. Ship owners, ships' captains, shipbuilders, and their employees formed a good proportion of the population, and the wealth of those times is evident in many of the town's fine old houses. It was the second largest port of registry in the country in the late 1870s and early 1880s, just before the decline of shipbuilding.

From the early days of settlement, Yarmouth harbour was a base for fishing vessels and fish processing. A visitor in 1915 observed that in the previous season nearly two million pounds of fresh lobster and fourteen thousand cases of canned lobster had been exported, saying, "A thousand men are engaged on this immediate coast fishing for lobster and cod, their fleet consisting of over half a hundred motorboats." The town still has an impressive fishing fleet.

A birds-eye view of Yarmouth made in 1889 shows the harbour's many warehouses and wharves, with ships of all sorts and sizes in port. It also identifies the

Unloading the catch in Yarmouth Harbour, ca. 1940. Note the lobster traps on the wharf.

various businesses that brought prosperity to the town. Raw materials for manufacturing were easily imported, factories grew up, and finished goods were exported through the harbour. Trading vessels were kept busy, and in the early twentieth century quantities of lumber were shipped to South America.

Because of its proximity to the United States, Yarmouth became the Nova Scotia base for a series of companies offering transport to various American ports. The Yarmouth Steamship Company, established in the 1880s, ran between Yarmouth and Boston, and brought American tourists to the area. Since then, a series of companies have provided ferry services to and from New England ports. Once operated as a passenger service in conjunction with the railways, more recently the ferries to and from Portland, Maine, have transported cars and commercial vehicles. Presently the ferry is the subject of controversy because of high operating expenses, low traffic, and demands for government subsidies. It is now scheduled to run between Yarmouth and Bar Harbor, Maine.

The lighthouse at Cape Forchu is a major attraction for visitors. The original building stood on the rocky cape with a dramatic view of the Gulf of Maine, St.

Marys Bay, and the entrance to the Bay of Fundy. It was replaced in 1961 by the present structure in the same location, which was automated in 1993. The site is now owned by the Municipality of Yarmouth County and operated by the Friends of the Yarmouth Light. One of the former lightkeeper's houses now serves in summer as a museum and café, while another is a gift shop.

ST. MARYS BAY

As the main highway begins to turn towards the Bay of Fundy, the scenic trailways signs for the Lighthouse Route make way for those of the Evangeline Trail. The first part of the journey runs along the shores of St. Marys Bay which is enclosed by Digby Neck, Long Island, and Brier Island. When Champlain first explored the southwest coast of Nova Scotia, he identified *"la baye saincte Marie"* as a suitable harbour where de Mons's expedition might moor their vessel before setting out to look for a permanent settlement site. The party sailed to the bay, the ship dropped anchor, and the adventurers began to explore the surrounding land.

While ashore on Digby Neck, one member of the expedition, a priest by the name of Aubry, left his sword behind. Going back to retrieve it, he became lost in the woods. When he failed to return, de Mons sent out a search party, but there was no sign of him, and he was given up for dead. After seventeen days, some crew members who had gone to fish in the Bay of Fundy saw a figure on the shore waving a hat on the end of a long stick. It was Aubry, who had wandered across the peninsula, barely surviving on plants and berries; he was eager to be rescued and brought back to the ship.

After spending about three weeks in St. Marys Bay without finding a suitable spot for their trading post, de Mons and Champlain took a smaller vessel to explore the Bay of Fundy. They found what seemed a good settlement site, sent a message back, and their ship left St. Marys Bay to join them. Their journey continues in a later chapter (see Bay of Fundy: Annapolis Basin, p. 95).

The Mi'kmaq remained alone in this area until exiled Acadians returned and, in 1768, land was surveyed on the southeastern shore to establish the Township (later known as the District) of Clare. This French-speaking community has grown over the centuries to become the centre of Acadian culture in the province. Like the neighbouring communities, the day-to-day life of the residents has been focussed on the fishery, shipbuilding, and related businesses. The schools and churches were important to the families that chose to stay in the area and to maintain and grow their distinct culture as Acadians.

The coast here does not have deep estuaries like those on the South Shore. In the little coves and estuaries, with their protecting breakwaters which sheltered fishing boats and merchant vessels, many wharves and shipyards were established. An early nineteenth-century traveller noted, "Their labour is divided between sea and land, they build their own shallops…and in these vessels they carry on fisheries to a limited extent off the provincial shores, or transport their agricultural produce to the market in their commercial capital, Saint John, New Brunswick."

Today, the economy on the bay is based on the sea rather than the land. A string of fishing villages extends from Cape St. Marys to St. Bernard. In a few generations, the Acadians in this region turned themselves from subsistence farmers to successful fishers.

The most striking landmarks in these villages are the impressive churches, built by the parishioners. The most magnificent one stands in the village of Pointe de l'Église (Church Point). Église Sainte-Marie is one of the largest wooden buildings in North America, measuring fifty-eight metres in length, with proportional transepts, and a spire rising fifty-six metres from the floor, topped by a cross that adds over a metre and a half to its height. No longer functioning as a church, it is being developed as an interpretive centre.

Cape St. Marys

The rugged headland of Cape St. Marys lies in the community of Mavillette, established in the early 1800s by descendants of the first Acadians to come to the bay. The harbour below the cliff shelters a prosperous fleet of small fishing vessels, protected by breakwaters. The first lighthouse was built above the harbour in 1868, replaced at the turn of the century, and then again, in 1965, by the present lighthouse.

Meteghan

The little harbour at Meteghan is one of the busiest in the District of Clare. The Mi'kmaq named the area Mitihikan, thought to mean "blue rocks," and the name has persisted in its present form.

Among the founders of the village of Meteghan was Prudent Robichaud, whose father had been a leading member of the community at Port Royal. Prudent, already an old man, came with his family to Meteghan in 1785. His descendants still live in the community. Other Acadian families who accompanied him began to farm the land around Meteghan River. The newcomers established subsistence farms, gradually turning their hands to fishing. Both the mouth of the Meteghan River and a little point of land at Meteghan provided sheltered mooring for fishing boats.

Fishing boats on the stocks at a Meteghan boatyard.

A flourishing shipbuilding industry grew up in Meteghan during the 1800s, and towards the end of the century a dry dock was established. Among the many vessels built here were a naval training schooner, HMCS *Venture*, launched in 1937, and wooden minesweepers for use during the Second World War. Smaller vessels were made for fishing, but the demand for wooden ships decreased rapidly in the twentieth century. A replica of the clipper ship *Flying Cloud*, launched in 1966, was the last large ship to be built here, and today the shipyard is closed. Instead, Meteghan harbour is home to a large fishing fleet that brings in a profitable catch of lobster, cod, crab, herring, and other species which are processed locally.

At Meteghan River, a similar story unfolded, but with a different outcome. A wharf was built at the river mouth, and by the 1840s, ships were mooring here. Towards the end of the century locally built fishing schooners brought their catch into port for processing, and large commercial schooners could be seen under construction at shipyards on both sides of the harbour. Shipyards began closing in the 1920s and the fishery was in a slump. There was no longer a demand for large wooden schooners, and fewer fishing boats set out to sea.

This changed in 1934 when the A. F. Thériault boatyard opened and began building motorized fishing boats and other small vessels. In the 1970s, the Thériault yard built a wooden sailing ship, a replica of a privateer, *La Belle Province*. Today, a third generation of Thériaults operates the yard, which is now the only large shipbuilding operation in the District of Clare. An important part of the yard's business is the manufacture of lobster boats. They have also built ferries for the Long Island, LaHave, and Halifax services, fire and pilot boats, private yachts, and a variety of other craft.

Like their counterparts in neighbouring villages, the fishers of Meteghan River are busy in the lobster season, and at other times a variety of catches keeps the area's seafood processors busy. The largest processing company—Comeau Seafoods, established in 1946—is at Saulnierville. It markets a variety of products and provides employment for both fishers and fish processors.

Weymouth Harbour

Weymouth, now predominantly English-speaking, lies closer to the head of St. Marys Bay. Its harbour is formed by the estuary of the Sissiboo River. The river's name probably comes from a Mi'kmaw word, *sipu*, meaning "river," but a more interesting, though dubious, explanation is that the early French expedition of which Champlain was a member saw six owls, *six hibous*, while they were exploring the area.

At the mouth of the harbour is the small community of New Edinburgh, a fishing port established by Anthony Stewart and Samuel Gouldsbury, Loyalists of Scottish origin. They were joined by returning Acadians, and from early days the residents made their livings harvesting clams, fishing, and fish processing. The little harbour at New Edinburgh was home for many years to the Frank E. Davis Fish Plant and Cannery, which opened in 1903 and was the community's chief employer. Fishing boats still come and go in the harbour, and wharves are busy during the lobster season.

The town of Weymouth at the head of the harbour was originally known simply as Sissiboo. A few Acadian families came to the area after their return from exile, along with some New Englanders who came to Nova Scotia in the 1760s. Among them was the Strickland family from Weymouth in Massachusetts, who brought the name with them. Loyalists settlers from New England joined them in 1783 and developed the town. This group included Colonel James Moody, who had played an exciting role in the revolution as an intelligence agent, intercepting dispatches, escaping prison, and evading capture. He received a grant in Weymouth on which he established a farm. Well paid for his wartime services, Moody became one of the town's leading citizens, was colonel of its militia, and established a shipyard and lumber mills.

Like Shelburne, Weymouth was also home to a community of Black Loyalists and their families. These were former slaves who had won their freedom by joining the British military during the American Revolution. They worked in the town's shipyards, in lumber camps, and as domestic servants in times past.

Weymouth quickly grew into a prosperous shipbuilding town and an important trading port. In the 1800s, locally built ships carried lumber and other goods to the St. Lawrence River, up to the Great Lakes, to the United States, the West Indies, and Europe. In 1896, F. Fawes Smith established a pulp mill near the town, bringing further prosperity to the community. Meanwhile, inland on the Silver River, the Stehelin family was creating the lumbering settlement of New France, otherwise known as Electric City because water-powered generators provided electricity for street and domestic lighting, before local towns had electricity.

Lumber from the mill was initially hauled down by oxen to be exported from the company wharf at Weymouth. In 1897, the Stehelins built a wooden railroad, carrying goods and passengers to and from the harbour more efficiently. Fire destroyed the railroad in 1909, along with several businesses in the town.

Like other lumbering and shipbuilding towns, Weymouth suffered a decline in the early twentieth century. This was followed by another disastrous fire in 1929, which destroyed many homes and businesses. New industries started up, but Weymouth never regained its former prosperity. In the 1950s, two more fires destroyed businesses in the town.

Merchant ships no longer sail in and out of Weymouth's harbour. Today, kayakers and canoeists enjoy the scenery, and in the town, the Sissiboo Landing interpretive centre encapsulates the history of this once prosperous area.

Bay of Fundy

As this journey continues towards the northeast, we begin to appreciate the extraordinary majesty of the Bay of Fundy, with its exceptional high tides, which surge twice each day into its harbours and then retreat, leaving extensive mud flats where boats lie grounded until the tide turns. Champlain first explored and mapped what he called *"la Baie Française"* between 1604 and 1607. The Acadians who settled around the bay drained the marshes for farming, laying the foundation for all future agriculture in this area, and also built ships for trade with New Englanders.

During the nineteenth century, fishing, trading, and shipbuilding continued to support the population, and during the age of sail, hundreds of wooden ships were launched in small harbours around the bay. The built heritage—houses and churches—in this area still show off the carpentry skills of these shipbuilders.

DIGBY NECK, LONG ISLAND, AND BRIER ISLAND

"There she blows!" Many international summer visitors come to this remote part of Digby County and enjoy the whale-watching tours offered from several of its harbours. But how many Nova Scotians have taken the road along the far side of St. Marys Bay to visit Brier Island and see the variety of wildlife to be found there? This finger of land between the Bay of Fundy and St. Marys Bay is an extension of North Mountain. It is cut through in two places by the Grand and Petit Passages—so named by Champlain during his voyage of exploration in 1604—which are crossed by ferries. Settlement began in the 1780s, when Loyalists established fishing communities on several little harbours.

Sandy Cove Harbour in the 1930s, with houses looking across St. Marys Bay.

Sandy Cove

The road along Digby Neck passes through the village of Sandy Cove, where there are in fact two coves—one on the Fundy shore and one on St. Marys Bay, which is the site of the first settlement. Thomas Hamilton and John Dickson, who came with their families in the late 1770s, established a fishery and were joined by Loyalists who received land grants in 1788. They built their homes, cleared the land for farming, fished, and built up their communities.

Among the leading citizens were the Morehouse, Eldridge, Fountain, Harris, and Saunders families. Squire John Morehouse ran a sawmill on a brook running into the harbour, and the first ships built in Sandy Cove came from a small shipyard below his house. The Morehouse yard continued to produce wooden vessels until the end of the nineteenth century. Stephen Fountain, a blacksmith, made spikes, rudder irons, and other items for the mill and shipyard. John Squires Eldrige was a sea captain and built one of the village's oldest surviving homes in the 1840s. Most people then owned locally built boats with which they fished for cod, haddock, pollock, and halibut. Fish was dried along the shore and exported by the community's merchants, who imported goods to stock their stores. Before wharves were constructed in the harbour, vessels were pulled up on the beach.

Sandy Cove was the scene of a strange event in September 1863. A boy walking on the beach found a man, apparently a castaway from a passing ship, lying helpless on the shore. Both of his legs had been recently amputated, and the stumps were still bandaged. He was also suffering from cold and exposure. He was taken in by the boy's family and subsequently cared for in other homes in the village, the subject of curious visitors. He was unable—or unwilling—to speak and appeared not to understand English or several other languages. When his rescuers tried to find out who he was, he made a sound that they interpreted as "Jerome." After a while the people of Sandy Cove judged from his appearance that he was of Mediterranean origin and probably a Catholic, and they arranged for him to be transferred across St. Marys Bay to Meteghan, perhaps relieved to be rid of their strange uninvited guest. A rock near the place where he was found is known today as Jerome's rock.

Fishing, trading, and shipbuilding continued to sustain the community's economy during the nineteenth century. Most families ran subsistence farms to provide food for the family, and some captains had additional sources of income. Three vessels were built before 1850, and twenty-two more in the next thirty years. The Sandy Cove harbour was busy with fishing boats and merchant ships.

Towards the end of the century both shipbuilders and merchant seamen suffered a decline in business. Fishing, including a traditional weir fishery, has continued despite ups and downs.

The road continues along Digby Neck to Long Island, separated from the mainland by Petit Passage. Champlain had noted strong tides there that made it "very dangerous for vessels that were prepared to risk taking it." Today, the *Petit Princess* carries passengers the short distance from East Ferry to Tiverton's little harbour on Long Island.

Tiverton was founded in 1785. It used to be known simply as Petit Passage until its name was officially changed to that of an English town in Devonshire, the birthplace of schoolteacher Thomas Mildon.

Fishing was always the mainstay of Tiverton's economy: in the nineteenth century when its fishing boats operated in the Bay of Fundy and offshore grounds, wharves and fish stores lined the shore. Like other fishing communities, Tiverton suffered periods of hardship in the early years of the twentieth century but has revived with tourism. When the lobster season is over, fishing boats take summer visitors on whale-watching cruises from Tiverton Harbour.

The twin harbours of Freeport and Westport on either side of Grand Passage, at the far end of Long Island, form the final link in the route to Brier Island, the westernmost point of North Mountain. Although Champlain had explored the area in 1604, no attempt at settlement was made for more than a century.

After the American Revolution, Loyalists settled around Freeport harbour, which became a prosperous fishing village and seaport. The shipyards produced large trading vessels that sailed to distant destinations. Wharves lined the harbour and, at its height, the community had around one thousand residents.

Today, the ferry across Grand Passage docks in Brier Island's Westport, which was first settled by Judah Rice and his wife, Sarah, David Welch and his family, and Robert and Moses Morrell. They were joined in the 1780s by a group of Loyalists, and took up the traditional occupations of fishing, shipbuilding, and merchant shipping, trading with the Acadian settlements across the bay.

Westport's most famous former resident lived there for only eight years, from the age of eight, when he arrived on Brier Island with his family in 1852. His father made boots for locals, and young Joshua Slocombe worked in his shop. He watched the comings and goings of the ships in the harbour and could not wait to leave home and join them. When he was fourteen, he ran away and signed on as cabin boy and cook for a fishing schooner, but was soon home again. Two years later Joshua left home for Halifax and was taken on as an ordinary seaman on a trading vessel leaving for Dublin. In 1898, after many years at sea and many adventures, he completed the first solo circumnavigation of the globe in his sloop *Spray*. Slocum, as he was later known, never returned to live in Westport, but a monument near the bootmaker's shop commemorates his exploits. Naturally, one of the ferries across Grand Passage was named the Joshua Slocum.

Originally, the residents of Freeport and Westport rowed their own boats between the two harbours, but in 1817, Robert Morrell's son, George, operated the first ferry linking Brier and Long Islands. This service was maintained over the years and is now a provincial government operation, with a mechanized car-carrying vessel. The current ferry, built in the Thériault shipyards across the bay, is named *Margaret's Justice*. The name honours Margaret Davis of Brier Island, who walked to Halifax and back in 1828 to successfully defend her rights in a property dispute with her neighbour.

The population of both communities decreased in the early twentieth century, but today, most people who live there year-round make their living by commercial fishing. Birdwatchers come to enjoy the variety of species that frequent the island, and tourism has become an important part of the economy.

ANNAPOLIS BASIN

The road back from Long Island, along Digby Neck, joins the main highway at the town of Digby, which faces the Annapolis Basin and the mouth of the Annapolis River. This area is where the first European settlement was established, and it is here where much of the struggle for control of the colony, between Britain and France, was played out.

In 1604, Pierre Dugua de Mons's expedition, which included Samuel de Champlain, was looking for a place to establish a fur-trading post. The expedition sailed through a gap in the coast and came to what Champlain described as "one of the finest harbours that I have seen anywhere on these coasts, where two thousand vessels could moor safely. The entrance is eight hundred paces wide: then you enter a harbour that is two leagues long and one league wide, that I have named Port Royal." He had no idea that this harbour would witness so many of the twists and turns of Nova Scotia's history.

The Port Royal Habitation

Near the head of the Annapolis Basin, the reconstructed Port Royal Habitation brings to life the earliest French settlement in Acadie. Visitors are invited to imagine themselves back in the years 1605–1607 when de Mons's voyagers were living in what they called the Habitation of Port Royal. They had left their initial settlement site on the far side of the Bay of Fundy after a disastrous winter, and returned to Port Royal, where they selected a sheltered spot behind Goat Island, protected by North Mountain. They brought the timbers from their abandoned settlement and built a group of buildings that enclosed a courtyard, giving them security against the weather and possible attack. De Mons returned to France to seek support for the settlement, leaving forty-five men in the Habitation, among them Champlain, who took a leading role in the community.

They were befriended by the Mi'kmaq in the region, in particular by Chief Membertou who ensured that the newcomers learned necessary skills to help them adapt to their new environment. The Mi'kmaq and the French remained on good terms, sharing social occasions and each other's cultures.

In 1606 a French vessel brought new settlers, led by Jean de Poutrincourt. Among them were Poutrincout's son, Charles de Biencourt, Claude de LaTour and his son Charles, the apothecary Louis Hébert, and Marc Lescarbot, a Parisian lawyer, scholar, and poet.

Champlain and Poutrincourt used Port Royal Harbour as a base for expeditions to continue exploring the coast of North America. On their return from one

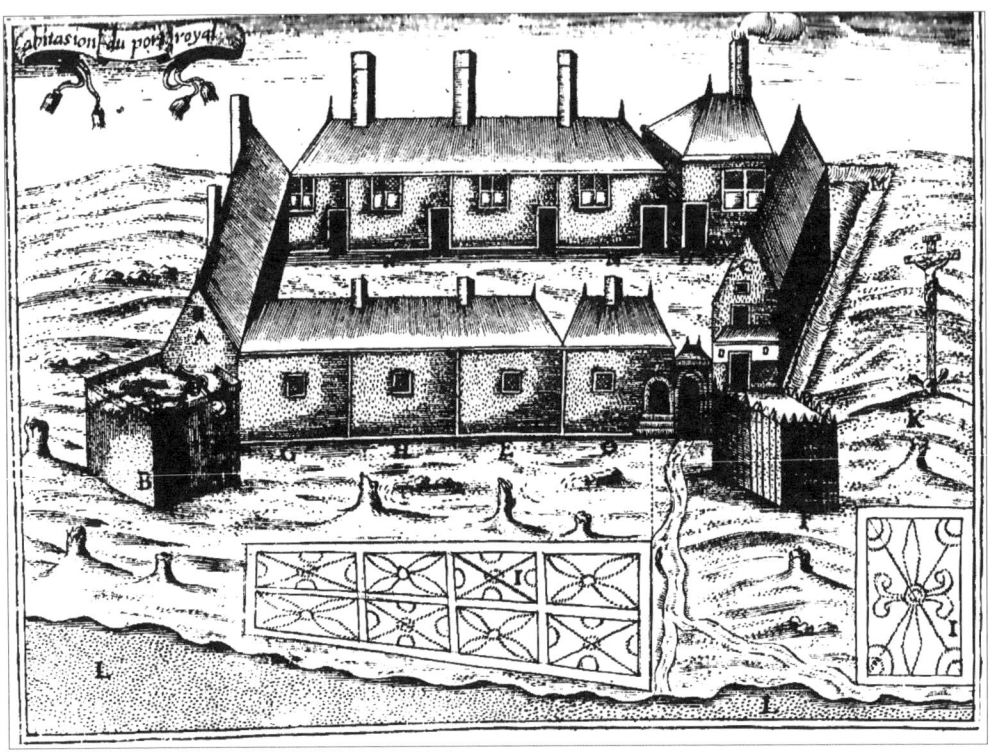

Champlain's drawing of the Habitation at Port Royal as it was in 1607.

of these voyages, they were welcomed by the first dramatic performance in North America—*Le Théâtre de Neptune*, written and directed by Lescarbot.

The settlers created gardens around the Habitation, and Poutrincourt began to cultivate wheat on the point where Annapolis Royal now stands. He planted orchards and built a gristmill on the Lequille River. Under his leadership, good relations were maintained with the Mi'kmaq, and the fur trade developed. The first vessel to be built in the Annapolis Basin was launched at Port Royal. Champlain initiated the Order of Good Cheer, whose members took turns preparing a lavish meal for their fellows to help them through the long winter. Membertou was often a guest at their table, and one young man from the Habitation spent some time living with the Mi'kmaq.

The Habitation was becoming firmly established when political scheming in France brought an end to de Mons's trading licence. The settlers were forced to leave, and they sailed away reluctantly from Port Royal in the summer of 1607, leaving the Habitation in Membertou's care.

The reconstructed Habitation, now a National Historic Site.

Poutrincourt, who had been granted seigneurial rights in the Port Royal area, returned in 1610 with his son, his nephew Charles de LaTour, and a new contingent of recruits. Membertou and his people had taken good care of the Habitation. Poutrincourt sent back furs, but he still needed to enlist further financial support, so the following year he returned to France. Unfortunately, in his absence, a raiding party from New England destroyed the Habitation while the men were working in the fields at the head of the Basin. On his return in March 1614, Poutrincourt found the colonists starving amidst the ruins of their buildings. After this setback, he was forced to abandon the settlement and take most of the men back to France. Charles de Biencourt, Charles de LaTour, and a few others remained behind and attempted to revive the trading post, but after a short time they transferred their attention to the Cape Sable area.

The construction of the replica Habitation based on Champlain's drawing was begun in 1939 and completed in 1941. Today, the site is managed by Parks Canada;

costumed interpreters encourage visitors to experience the site as if it were still a flourishing fur-trading post.

Port Royal and Annapolis Royal

In the 1620s, a Scot, Sir William Alexander, devised a grandiose scheme to expand British territory in North America by developing a colony in what he proposed to call Nova Scotia (New Scotland). Since the French had abandoned Port Royal, in 1629 Alexander's Scottish garrison built a fort, called Charlesfort, at the site where Poutrincourt had cultivated wheat. However, France regained authority in Acadie two years later, and in 1632, the Scottish fort was taken over by a small French garrison. When Charles de Menou d'Aulnay took control of Acadie in 1636, he brought the settlers from LaHève to make Port Royal his centre of operations and refurbished the fort overlooking the harbour. For several summers, ships brought new recruits to the little town that began to grow up around it.

D'Aulnay and Charles de LaTour soon renewed their quarrel over control of trade in Acadie. Skirmishes took place at Port Royal in 1640, and three years later, LaTour raided the settlement, burned the mill, killed some cattle, and carried off goods. These confrontations wasted energy and resources that would have been better spent developing the colony.

D'Aulnay drowned in a canoe accident in 1650, and for the rest of the century, his successors at Port Royal were subject to attacks from New England as the British strove to expand into French territory. In 1654, an expedition from Massachusetts sailed into the harbour and captured the fort, bringing Acadie under British rule. France regained control of its territory in 1667, and by the time Intendant de Meulles visited in 1686, the population of Port Royal was consolidated around its church and fort. The residents were still dependent for many essentials on imported supplies, and British merchants set up stores in the town, stocked by trading vessels from New England.

Some Acadians from Port Royal moved out of town and established farms by draining the marshes at the head of the harbour. A cluster of houses built on the northern shore by the Melanson, Belliveau, Robicheaux, and la Liberté families formed the Melanson village, now a National Historic Site. Their houses stood on the slopes overlooking their fields and the water. From there, they would witness the comings and goings of fishing boats, trading ships, and vessels of war.

Hostilities broke out again between England and France, and in 1690 a raiding party led by Sir William Phips seized the town of Port Royal. It remained in British hands until 1697, when Acadie was once more accorded to France. By this time, many more Acadians had left the beleaguered town for more peaceful rural areas, and the population consisted mainly of French soldiers and administrators. Work began on a new fort overlooking the harbour, but before it could be completed, England and France were again at war, and Port Royal was caught up in the strife.

In 1704 raiders from New England attacked the farming settlements, sparing the town, but three years later Port Royal was attacked twice. New England troops dug trenches on the nearby farmland as a base for their attack, and although the raiders were repelled, many houses were destroyed. In 1710, after a final siege, Port Royal fell to the British for the last time—and with it, the rest of Acadie.

British troops quickly moved into the new capital of Nova Scotia, renaming it Annapolis Royal in honour of Queen Anne. They constructed Fort Anne on the site of the former Scottish and French forts at the head of the Annapolis Basin. Nevertheless, for many years the town continued to suffer attacks by Indigenous and Acadian raiders.

In 1746, ships carrying French soldiers sailed into the Annapolis Basin, expecting to meet naval reinforcements from France, led by the duc d'Anville. But the few ships from d'Anville's fleet that made it as far as Halifax had returned to France. Without this support, the would-be attackers retreated. When Halifax became the capital of Nova Scotia in 1749, Annapolis Royal ceased to be the focus of attention. A significant Acadian farming population remained in the surrounding area until the Expulsion of 1755, when thirty-two families were herded onto the British vessel *Pembroke*. She sailed from the Basin bound for North Carolina, but the prisoners seized control of the ship and took her to the St. John River, where they burned the vessel and escaped to safety.

With the Acadian farmers gone, the authorities in Halifax feared for their food supply and needed to establish a stable loyal population. Annapolis and Granville townships were created in 1760, one each side of the Annapolis Basin, and a ship, the *Charming Molly*, brought a new contingent of settlers into the harbour.

During the American Revolution, Annapolis Royal was raided and looted by privateers, but the end of the war saw a renewal of the town as its population was increased by shiploads of Loyalists, including Free Blacks who had fought on the British side.

The wide tidal range at the head of the Annapolis Basin made ideal conditions for shipbuilding, and many vessels were launched here during the nineteenth century. The opening of the Windsor and Annapolis Railway in 1869 made the town a commercial hub for the region and several industries started up. In the 1880s, steamships began to come to its piers. Business was brisk until the railway was extended to the deeper harbours of Digby and Yarmouth in the 1890s, when businesses closed and the population decreased.

The ferry that had linked Granville and Annapolis throughout the nineteenth century was replaced in 1921 by a bridge, which in turn gave way to a causeway where the Annapolis Royal Tidal Generating Station was installed in 1984. This method of obtaining power from the Fundy tides is now controversial, as conservationists claim it damages fish stocks.

Tourism is now a major part of the economy in this region where so many events of Canada's colonial past took place. Fort Anne was designated as a National Historic Park (later, National Historic Site) in 1917 and nearby Port Royal followed in 1925, followed by the reconstruction that was completed in 1941. The Sinclair Inn/Farmers Hotel National Historic Site, on St. George Street, incorporates a former Acadian structure built in 1708–1710 by Jean-Baptiste Souillard, a gunsmith for the French garrison. It is now an amalgamation of two buildings, with later additions. As well as offering lodging, it once served as meeting hall for Canada's first Masonic Lodge, and includes a painted room dating from about 1840. The Sinclair Inn now operates as a museum.

Digby

At the southwestern end of the basin is the town of Digby, best known to many travellers as the terminal for the ferry that carries cars and commercial vehicles across the Bay of Fundy to Saint John, New Brunswick. Just to the north of the town is the narrow entrance to the Annapolis Basin, known as Digby Gut. The tides surging through this opening have always presented challenges for shipping, and especially for sailing vessels.

After the American Revolution, Rear Admiral Sir Thomas Digby brought ships successfully through the channel, carrying Loyalist settlers from New York, including Free Blacks. They disembarked at a spot at the western end of the basin, not far from the entrance. A small community of Planters had previously settled here and called it Conway, but the newcomers received permission to rename it Digby in honour of the man who had led them safely to British territory. It became the administrative centre of the county of the same name.

Digby lies between the harbour known as the Racquette and a larger cove, the Joggins. The town was laid out in the grid pattern typical of colonial settlements, and quickly developed into an important fishing port. The nineteenth century was a time of prosperity; the fishery became a major industry and the port was renowned for scallops and salted smoked herring, known as Digby chicks. Shipyards were

Maritime Fish Corporation from Warne's, Digby *shows the Robertson fish processing plant and fishing boats, 1927.*

established on both the Racquette and the Joggins, and lumber was a major export. Merchant vessels constantly sailed in and out through Digby Gut, carrying fish and lumber and bringing in goods from the West Indies and elsewhere.

By the end of the nineteenth century, shipbuilding was on the decline, but commercial shipping continued as steamships slowly replaced sailing vessels. The ferry service across the Bay of Fundy was instituted in 1894, in collaboration with the Dominion Atlantic Railway, whose line provided a link between Halifax and western Nova Scotia. By 1895 a railway wharf was bringing freight and passengers to the ferry terminal, and this helped the growth of services, such as hotels, to accommodate travellers. Today, trains no longer run, but the ferry provides a valuable link for private and commercial vehicles.

Digby is home port to an important fleet of scallop fishing boats, and has an annual Scallop Days Festival.

Clementsport

Also on the Annapolis Basin, between Digby and Annapolis Royal on the old highway (Route 1) is the town of Clementsport, at the mouth of Moose River. Some Planter families settled here in the 1760s, but the community grew in 1783–1784 with the arrival of Loyalists from New York and some disbanded German mercenaries. Many of the Loyalists were of Dutch origin. Led by Douwe Ditmars, they received land around the harbour, while the Germans established farms inland on what was known as the Hessian line.

Clementsport became home to sawmills and shipyards, and for a time, to another important industry, when iron ore was found nearby. The ironworks and blast furnace were started up in 1825. A water-powered foundry produced stoves and other household items. The finished products were shipped from Clementsport Harbour. The supply of ore proved to be short-lived, however, and operations ceased in 1863. Mining resumed briefly in 1872 and in the ten weeks when the furnace was operating, 163 tons of pig iron were produced and loaded onto ships for Boston. Today, traces of the village's industrial past can still be seen on the shores of the Basin.

Among Clementsport's early settlers was a family by the name of Rawding. Fourteen members of the Rawding family, beginning with Joseph, born in 1771, served as sea captains, and a monument in the town lists their names and reads as follows: "These sea captains all resident in this locality and members of the one family roamed the seven seas for 150 years and had under their command some of the largest vessels then existing." Their names recall an exciting period of the history of what is now a quiet residential community.

MINAS BASIN

Our exploration continues through the Annapolis Valley, past Cape Blomidon to the Minas Basin, with its farms, vineyards, and orchards. This was the scene of important events in Nova Scotia's history.

For the Mi'kmaq this is a very special area, associated with their archetype, Kluskap, who lived at Cape Blomidon, at the entrance to the Minas Basin. To account for the physical characteristics of the Basin, many different stories are told of Kluskap and his power over nature. According to one tale, Kluskap had asked Beaver to build a dam across from Blomidon so he could take a bath. Beaver refused to remove the dam, so Kluskap asked Whale to flip his tail to break it. The water rushed through the breach, creating the high tides which are characteristic of the bay.

In today's terms, the Basin is a body of water with a narrow entrance between the projecting spur of Cape Split on the south side and Partridge Island on the north, through which strong currents flow. Long before Europeans came here, the Mi'kmaq gathered in summer to perform spiritual ceremonies, exchange news, conduct business, celebrate marriages, feast, and tell stories. In the area around Cape Split, they collected chalcedony and agate, with which they made tools and weapons.

When the Acadians began to migrate beyond the immediate vicinity of Port Royal in the 1680s, they made their way to the Basin, where they settled around the river mouths that served as harbours. They drained the marshes for farmland but depended on ships to trade their own produce for supplies from Port Royal or, frequently, from merchants in Boston. Small ships could come into the harbour entrances at high tide, but because of the range of the tides, were grounded a few hours later. Goods were transported either in small boats or by foot across the mud flats, before the vessels sailed out again at high water.

In 1755, the Minas Basin was the scene of one of the most infamous events in Canadian history. During the Seven Years' War, disputes over the boundary between Nova Scotia and New France intensified, and fearing an uprising, Governor Lawrence ordered the Acadians to be deported. That autumn, British ships anchored offshore, and carried over two thousand people from the surrounding communities into exile.

In the 1760s, would-be settlers arrived from New England to take over the farmland, and established themselves as fishers, shipbuilders, merchants, and tradesmen. During the nineteenth century, many fortunes were made by merchants, shipbuilders, and ship owners in this area with the export of raw materials, such as gypsum and lumber, and the importation of manufactured goods.

Today, commercial shipping has been replaced by other forms of transport. Farms and vineyards bring prosperity to the area and attract many visitors who come by road. Ferries no longer cross the Basin, and the little ports that were once the lifeline of communities are no more.

Grand Pré, Horton, Mud Creek, and Port Williams

The largest area reclaimed by the Acadians in the seventeenth century was Grand Pré, the "great meadow" between the Cornwallis and the Gaspereau estuaries. Grand Pré village was built on the ridge overlooking the fields. Many people who could not locate the Minas Basin on a map have read or heard of Longfellow's poem *Evangeline*, which is the story of two mythical Acadians, Evangeline and Gabriel, deported from Grand Pré. This story of love and loss has iconic status in Acadian culture. The Deportation Cross can be found at Hortonville, at the mouth of the Gaspereau River. While the French and the British were vying for control of the colony, Governor Lawrence asked the Acadians to sign an Oath of Allegiance to the English Crown. A delegation of deputies went to Halifax to negotiate with the authorities, but the men were imprisoned when their discussions reached an impasse. Soon after, orders were given to remove all Acadians from Nova Scotia. At

The Deportation Cross stands by the place from which the Acadians were expelled from villages on the Minas Basin.

Grand Pré, the men and boys were imprisoned in the church to await deportation, leaving their farms untended, while their anxious womenfolk packed up what they could salvage from their homes, and tried to comfort each other and their frightened children. Early in October 1755 they were all herded onto boats in the harbour and taken to the waiting larger ships that would carry them away from their homeland. Some family members were separated and sent to different destinations as far apart as France and the Carolinas.

In 1760 ships carrying settlers sailed into this same harbour to take up the governor's offer of land that had been left vacant after the Deportation. Their passengers disembarked at the spot whence the Acadians had departed, known as Horton Landing. Near their landing place, streets were laid out for the town of Horton, the administrative centre of Horton township. As expected, these New England Planters assumed ownership of the abandoned farms at Grand Pré and brought them back into cultivation. Some also were involved with the fishery, and by the end of the century cod and salmon were being processed in Horton. The Gaspereau River was described as "navigable for any vessel that can lay aground there being seven fathoms at high water. At low water the lands are in a manner dry." Both fishing boats and small merchant vessels used the harbour.

Horton did not remain the centre of the township, as the settlers soon began to move away to live on their farms or to form communities farther west. In the early nineteenth century, Fowler's Inn at Horton catered to passing travellers and served as a post house, but today all that remains of the original settlement are the few streets and scattered houses of what is now called Hortonville.

Many of Horton's original settlers moved to where Mud Creek joins the Cornwallis River. Among the first were three brothers, Simeon, Nathan, and Jehiel DeWolf who soon became prominent citizens, and owned much of the property in the new community. Mud Creek soon replaced Horton as the commercial and social centre of the township. Some ships were built and the mouth of the creek became a trading port, providing a harbour for small merchant vessels that sailed as far away as the West Indies.

During the American Revolution, raids by privateering vessels were a constant threat to coastal communities, so Horton Township established a militia for its defence. In May 1781, an American privateer suddenly appeared in the basin from behind Blomidon and, taking workmen who were loading a ship by surprise, the raiders seized the vessel. Local resident William Bishop and some companions came to the owner's assistance, but the raiders sailed the ship away, along with the defenders. A neighbour, Benjamin Belcher, alerted members of the militia and they sailed out in pursuit of the privateers. The Americans had not reckoned with the strong incoming tide and were foiled in their attempt to leave. The skirmish that ensued—the Battle of Blomidon—resulted in the defeat of the raiders and the capture of three American ships.

Nathan DeWolf's son Elisha became a prominent merchant, with interests in Mud Creek's trading vessels. It is said that the name of the village was changed to Wolfville because his granddaughters were embarrassed to tell their classmates at boarding school that they came from Mud Creek. The local postmaster, Elisha Junior, approached the Postmaster General and the request for the name change was granted in 1830.

Like other small Nova Scotia harbours, Wolfville prospered during much of the nineteenth century when shipbuilding and merchant shipping flourished. The waterfront around the creek became the centre of the community's economy, with wharves and warehouses, outfitters, and a variety of businesses. Two factors put an end to the town's function as a trading port: when the Dominion Atlantic Railway was built in 1868, it cut across the creek, isolating the inner harbour from the sea and reducing the space available for ships to anchor. Then larger steamships began to replace sailing vessels, and merchant shipping was no longer viable in Wolfville's small harbour.

For many years, a ferry service linked Wolfville with the north shore of the basin. The last ferry boat was the MV *Kipawo*, named for Kingsport, Parrsboro, and Wolfville, the three ports it served. This service stopped at the time of the Second World War. Today, the wharf at "the world's smallest harbour," at Waterfront Park, with its pleasant view across the Basin, is little-used. The former inner harbour area has become an attractive park, with little resemblance to the hive of commercial activity that once surrounded it. The pond is the only relic of the former creek.

Wolfville today is home to Acadia University, and is surrounded by farms, vineyards, and wineries. The town's maritime history is largely forgotten.

Port Williams stands on the far side of the Cornwallis River, the largest of the tidal rivers that flow into the Minas Basin from the west. The river was called Grand Habitant by the Acadians who created pasture on the marshes and built their houses on a rise of land that they called La Petite Côte. Boats pulled up on what was known as Boudreau's Bank, near Starrs Point. Their farms met the same fate as others in the area at the time of the Deportation.

The New England Planters settled on what became known as Cornwallis Township, where a town plot was laid out at the mouth of the river. They built a wharf and established a ferry to link the town with Horton Township, across the river.

It had been assumed that the town at the river mouth would remain the administrative centre for the township, but it was not long before its residents became frustrated by their isolation and began to move away. Meanwhile a more viable settlement was developing at Terrys Creek, at the head of navigation, now known as Port Williams. A bridge is thought to have been built there as early as 1780 to provide better communications with neighbouring communities to the south.

During the nineteenth century Port Williams served the surrounding agricultural area. In mid-century Joseph Howe remarked that trading vessels glimpsed over the top of the dykes as they came up the river appeared to be sailing on dry land: "Nothing can be more novel to the eyes of a person unaccustomed to this inland navigation, than seeing the hull and sails of a vessel, often before the water on while she reclines; it is a strange but not unpleasing commingling of Trade and Agriculture."

By 1870, three master mariners and ship owners were operating out of Port Williams, and others served as seamen on their vessels. When the age of sail came to an end at the turn of the century, residents turned their hand to other activities. Diversified businesses in Port Williams are now predominantly based on local agriculture, and trucks have replaced ships for transport. It is still fascinating to watch the tide rising or falling while eating at a riverside restaurant.

Avon River Estuary: Windsor, Hantsport, and Avondale

Turning inland from the Minas Basin, the road leads towards Windsor, and to a hill where Fort Edward overlooks the confluence of the Avon and St. Croix Rivers, two important travel routes for the Mi'kmaq between the lakes inland, and the place they called Pesekitk. This was an important meeting place where trade and ceremony were conducted, and shellfish and pelagic fish were harvested from the sea.

The Acadians who came to the area in the early eighteenth century adapted the name to Pisiquid and established family settlements on the rivers. Vessels from Port Royal or New England sailed in with imported goods to supplement the produce from their farms. During the Deportation, four transport vessels moored in the estuary and carried more than one thousand Acadians from Pisiquid into exile.

In the second half of the eighteenth century, well-to-do citizens from Halifax began to acquire land and establish homes, farms, and businesses at what was officially named Windsor in 1764. Two early residents, Moses and Gideon Delesdernier, soon set up a packet-boat service, carrying mail and passengers between Windsor and the Cumberland Basin.

The American Revolution brought Loyalist settlers to the area. The shipping industry was developing in Windsor by the 1790s. Much of the town's trade was with merchants bringing vessels from Boston into the Avon River, to take away lumber, agricultural produce, and gypsum from local quarries, and bring in manufactured goods.

Shipbuilding and merchant shipping grew rapidly in the early 1800s, and British demand for Nova Scotia's lumber during the Napoleonic Wars boosted the export industry. The growing trade in gypsum with the United States was often illicit as government-imposed duties on exports encouraged smuggling. As well as smugglers, a vessel from Windsor was engaged in privateering during the War of 1812.

An increasing number of coastal trading vessels, many of them also carrying travellers, made the port of Windsor an important centre for both commercial and passenger traffic. Ferries ran to Parrsboro and Saint John, and ships left Windsor for Eastport, Boston, New York, and other American ports. New industries came to the town, adding to the volume of traffic. Windsor had quickly become the second most important town in Nova Scotia, after the capital.

One of Windsor's early shipbuilders, John Smith, was operating before 1820, and his four sons followed him into the business in the 1830s. Bennett Smith became one of the area's most successful in this trade, owning a fleet of vessels that carried goods around the world. The demand for merchant ships grew, and censuses and business directories for the second half of the nineteenth century provide an impressive list of shipbuilders, ship owners, shipwrights, ships' carpenters, sail makers, painters, block-makers, caulkers, and carvers. The population also included merchants, ships' captains, and mariners.

The wooden shipbuilding era was already coming to an end in 1897, when a major fire destroyed much of the town. Homes and businesses were rebuilt, and trade continued, despite another fire in 1924. Lumber vessels still moored along the waterfront into the 1960s. At low tide they were buried deep in the red mud, waiting for high water to float them again so that they could continue their journey. But business was slowing, and the construction of a causeway at the mouth of the Avon River in 1970 closed it off to shipping. Windsor's harbour was no more.

Farther down the Avon estuary, the old road along the shore leads to Hantsport, where Churchill House recalls the importance of its harbour in the nineteenth century. Among the Planters in Falmouth Township was Colonel Henry Denny Denson who received a large tract of land that included the present town of Hantsport and the community of Mount Denson. In 1789 Edward Barker received an area around the mouth of the Halfway River—halfway between Windsor and Horton—as payment for services to the Crown, and expanded it by purchasing land from the Denson estate. Barker settled there with his family, and the settlement grew. It originally took its name from the river, but with the development of its harbour, it became known as Hantsport. The Barkers became leaders of the community. A small shipbuilding industry developed during the early nineteenth century, and Hantsport became a shipping point for exporting coal and gypsum.

In 1841, Edward Barker's son Robert sold a sixty-acre lot to a Hantsport merchant named Ezra Churchill. In that same year, Churchill entered the shipping business, buying shares in a small brigantine. He quickly expanded his holdings, commissioning the building of another brigantine and buying shares in several more vessels before starting to build ships himself. His first vessel, the *Morning*

Windsor at Low Tide. *Schooners on the mud flats by the wharves at Windsor in 1910.*

Star, was launched in 1856, and he went on to build large cargo ships. One of these, the *Hamburg*, is said to have been the largest three-masted barque ever built in Canada. Churchill's shipyard flourished and his fleet of merchant vessels traded in distant ports, making his business one of the most successful in Nova Scotia. After Ezra's death in 1874, his sons continued to run the shipyard and trading vessels, but the shipbuilding business was beginning to decline. The Churchill House, built by Ezra in 1860 for his son John, is still standing and is now a museum and community centre.

The Barkers, too, continued their connection with the sea, either as mariners or in the shipbuilding and supporting industries. One of Edward Barker's descendants remembers a family story about George Jackson Barker, Edward's grandson, who captained ships from Hantsport carrying cargoes along the Atlantic seaboard to the West Indies, with stops in Boston and New York. On one of his voyages in the mid– to late 1800s, he came upon a drifting vessel, part of what was known as the coal fleet that carried Nova Scotia's coal to export markets. He and some of his crew boarded her and found no sign of life. They were about to leave the abandoned ship when Jackson heard what sounded like a child's cry, from somewhere down below. He investigated and found a baby boy there. The infant was taken back to the Barker home in Hantsport, but Captain Barker was unable to trace the child's

Water Front, Hantsport, NS. A gypsum carrier operated by J. B. King and company is moored at the Hantsport wharf.

family. The mystery baby was named Peter Coalfleet, since he was found on a coal fleet vessel. Peter grew up in Hantsport and his descendants continue to live in the area.

Sometimes trading ships brought back exotic items that were unknown to many Nova Scotians, though familiar to us today. Another of Edward Barker's descendants, Clyde Barker, ran away to sea when he was ten years old, and served as a cabin boy for a short time. On one of his trips aboard a gypsum carrier out of Hantsport, after dropping off cargo in New York, the ship proceeded to the West Indies for the usual cargo of sugar, molasses, and rum, and they also took on a load of green bananas, which ripened on the way home and were much enjoyed by the people of Hantsport as an exotic fruit.

In the twentieth century, although ships were no longer built in Hantsport, the harbour remained busy with the export of gypsum. The company that operated the gypsum-loading facility was a major employer and contributor to the town's economy, with trains coming to the harbour from quarries near Windsor. The loading had to take place quickly, while the tide was high enough for the carriers to enter and leave the harbour. Demand for the product dropped off in the twenty-first century with a slump in the American housing market, and the quarry and the harbour's remaining maritime business were closed permanently in 2011.

The land along the St. Croix River had been farmed by Acadian families from the early eighteenth century until 1755. In 1760, some New England Planters received grants in the Township of Newport. They came ashore at Newport Landing, between the St. Croix and Kennetcook Rivers, in what is now Avondale. Land there formerly known as Thibodeau Village was granted to the Shaw family, who have farmed it ever since. In 2004 at the time of the Acadian World Congress, the Shaws welcomed members of the Thibodeau family back to their former home, re-establishing their historic link with the St. Croix River.

Newport Township's first known shipwright was Neil McCurdy, who came to the area in 1775, followed by others such as James and Nicholas Mosher and John Harvie, who altogether built 160 vessels. The last ship to be built there was the replica cargo schooner *Avon Spirit*, launched in 1996 as a souvenir of the area's former industry. Today, the Avon River Heritage Society hosts events of various kinds in Newport Landing's former boat shed, and operates a museum.

Two fine houses set side by side on the Avondale Road stand out in this small community. They were built by members of the Mounce family, descendants of Richard Mounce, who had married the daughter of one of Avondale's early settlers. Avondale was a busy trading port and the Mounces were prosperous ship-owners. Richard's son George ran away to sea as a young boy, signing on as a cabin boy on a schooner bound for England. He eventually became a successful sea captain and sailed around the world on merchant vessels. On his retirement, he returned to Avondale, where his brother, William, was still living. The two magnificent houses belonged to Richard's sons, Thomas and George. Thomas commissioned his splendid home as a wedding present for his bride. George, who lived on the adjoining property, upgraded his modest home to complement it.

Cobequid Bay

The road runs eastward from Avondale to Cobequid Bay at the upper end of the Minas Basin. The Mi'kmaq named the area We'kopekwitk, which the French adapted to Cobequit, and the English to Cobequid. It is worth taking a short detour to Burncoat Head, at the entrance to the bay, where the greatest tidal range occurs. There, at low tide, it is possible to stand on the seafloor and look up at the red cliffs where the high-water mark is sixteen metres overhead.

The wide tidal range creates tidal bores on the rivers flowing into the Cobequid Bay. This is a popular attraction on the Shubenacadie River, as the incoming tide forms impressive waves as it rushes up against the current. Running right across Nova Scotia, this river was a main travel route for the Mi'kmaq, who named it Sipekne'katik.

Maitland and Truro

In the early eighteenth century a number of Acadian families settled along the Noel Shore, between the Avon and Shubenacadie Rivers. After the Deportation, the township of Douglas was created on the west side of the Shubenacadie for the New Englanders who were brought in to replace them. The village of Maitland grew up at the mouth of a small tidal creek running into the estuary. Its little harbour was originally known simply as "the mouth of the river" but received its present name in 1838, in honour of the lieutenant governor, Sir Peregrine Maitland.

Among the first residents were New Englanders William Putnam, his son Caleb, and his stepfather, Luke Upham, who received a grant in 1771. They were joined by the Whidden family, David Whidden's son-in-law William Frieze, James Douglas, and others. The Whiddens were shipbuilders and they recognized the harbour at the river mouth as a good location. By the mid-nineteenth century, shipbuilding and merchant shipping had become the community's main occupation. Ambrose Church's 1871 county map identifies four shipyards and a sail loft, as well as associated "workshops" at Maitland. The large ships that were launched here, manned by men from the community, sailed all over the world.

In 1855 the shipbuilders were joined by William Dawson Lawrence, who had served his apprenticeship with a Dartmouth shipbuilder. He set up a shipyard in Maitland, where he built several vessels before embarking on the project for which he is famous. He drew up plans, created a half-model, and in September 1872 he laid the keel for what would be the largest wooden ship built in the Maritimes, and one of the largest ever built. The launching of the *William D. Lawrence* in 1874 must have been an impressive sight. She was a square-rigged trading vessel, in which Lawrence sailed with his family for three years. Lawrence continued to operate the ship profitably before he sold her in 1883. A monument to the ship stands on the grounds of Lawrence's house in Maitland, a National Historic Site which is now managed by the Nova Scotia Museum.

East of the Shubenacadie River, at the Salmon River estuary, is the town of Truro, which, today, has lost its connection to the shipbuilding and seaborne trade that helped establish the town. The Mi'kmaq who originally camped along the

Salmon River estuary were displaced in the 1880s for the construction of Truro's School of Agriculture. They were given a piece of land on King Street known as Christmas Crossing, but the reserve was later moved to land on the Halifax Road that is now the Millbrook reserve. On the four-lane highway outside Truro stands the Millbrook Cultural and Heritage Centre, overlooked by a giant statue of Kluskap.

The early days of European settlement begin with Matthieu Martin, a weaver by trade, who was granted the seigneury of Cobequit in 1689 in recognition of the fact that he was the first child to be born to a French family in Acadie. His tenants farmed the marshlands along the shore. Members of the community depended on trading for many of their necessities, and vessels came to Cobequid Bay bringing goods from France, Boston, and the West Indies.

In the 1740s, the Acadians of this area came under the influence of Abbé Jean-Louis LeLoutre, who encouraged them to resist British authority. By the time of the Expulsion, many of them had already left for French-controlled territory. Three British vessels sailed into the bay in September 1755, to carry away those who remained, seizing their property and burning their homes.

In 1761 a ship arrived with a group of Scottish-Irish immigrants from New Hampshire. They disembarked in the newly established township of Truro. Before the road and rail networks were developed, the community depended on trading vessels to bring in supplies, and to carry out exports, chiefly grain and lumber. These ships could only approach the shore at high tide and would have to wait for deep water before they could leave with their cargo. To load and unload at low tide, goods were hauled by ox carts over the mud flats.

A shipyard was established in Lower Truro by Charles Dickson, who launched his schooner *Charles* in 1787. Other shipbuilders followed; there were shipyards at Onslow, on the north side of the river, and at Old Barns, where James Crowe built many vessels in the 1800s. Dickson's ships traded in Britain and the West Indies. Three of them were chartered in 1796 to bring Jamaican Maroons to Halifax. Dickson's last ship came close to disaster at its launching. A crowd of people stood on its upper deck, including a band that was playing as the vessel moved down the slipway. It was evidently top-heavy so that as it entered the water, it tipped and almost rolled over. Luckily, it righted itself in time and disaster was averted.

Commercial activity at the river mouth decreased in the nineteenth century as Truro developed into an industrial town and an important road and rail junction.

CHIGNECTO SHORE

The road from Truro along the north shore of Cobequid Bay leads towards Cape Chignecto, which separates the Minas Basin from the Cumberland Basin. It runs past marshland once reclaimed by Acadian farmers and begins a winding trail along the coast, climbing steep hills, then descending into the villages at the mouth of each river.

Parrsboro

The largest of these estuaries is Parrsboro Harbour, at the southern end of a trail from the Cumberland Basin that was used for centuries by Mi'kmaw people and then by Acadians. This trail crosses the Chignecto Peninsula following River Hébert upstream to Halfway River and then downstream to Farrells River, reaching the Minas Basin shore at Partridge Island. The island was said to be Kluskap's grandmother's campsite and was also known as Kluskap's grandmother's cooking pot because the water around it appears to boil as the sea comes in at high tide. It was reputed to be an inexhaustible source of food. But the Mi'kmaq also came to Partridge Island to collect various types of stone used for making knives, tools, and weapons.

When Acadians settled along the northern shore of the Minas Basin in the early eighteenth century, they also used the old Mi'kmaw route to the community of Beaubassin on the Cumberland Basin. There was not a great deal of marshland along this part of the Minas shore to support farming, so the Acadians probably depended on the sea as much as the land for a living. In 1730, Jean Bourg and François Arsenau began a ferry service across the basin to the agricultural communities on the far shore.

In the early years of British settlement, after the Deportation, the small community on the shore behind Partridge Island was originally known by the same name. The island is joined to the mainland by a narrow neck of land that provides shelter for vessels. In the 1760s, a blockhouse was built on the hill overlooking the entrance to the Minas Basin. Land grants were issued in the early 1770s to Jonathan Crane and James Noble Shannon, who became leaders of the settlement on the strip of land below the fort.

With the departure of the Acadians there was nobody to run the ferry, so three men were offered land on condition they operate a service between Partridge Island harbour and Windsor. A settlement developed around the ferry, and trading vessels brought business to the community, where Shannon operated a store. In 1779, James Ratchford came to live there. A hard-headed entrepreneur, he also established a store and operated a hotel. He built a lumber mill and a shipyard on the west bank of the river in partnership with Shannon.

During the American Revolution, privateers raided the settlement, resulting on one occasion in the attacking ship being seized. Another raiding ship escaped, but some of its crew were killed or captured by the local militia. On another occasion, raiders seized a ferry boat, but it was quickly recaptured. A further American attack on the ferry was more successful, and Abijah Scott's boat was destroyed.

When peace returned, Ratchford continued to expand his business empire, and was joined by others who built sawmills on the river. As these industries developed, the population shifted up the river from Partridge Island to what was first known as Mill Village, and later became Parrsboro. The river was now busy with merchant vessels bringing goods into port from distant places, and newly launched ships lifting their sails in the estuary.

Ratchford was a hard character, like many entrepreneurs of his day who ran company stores. Lord Dalhousie, visiting Parrsboro in 1818, observed that "the whole population is extremely indebted to him; selling his goods at enormous profit he makes money of those who pay their accounts, and of those that do not he takes mortgages on their lands, takes that in payment." To his credit, he had established the infrastructure for Parrsboro's industrial and shipping prosperity.

The tidal currents at the entrance to the Minas Basin can be treacherous, and the lieutenant governor's journey to Parrsboro had almost ended in disaster. His party left Horton early in the afternoon on board "a very good sloop packet" for what should have been a quick journey, but the wind dropped when they were halfway across and they were caught in the strong current. Among the vice-regal party was Admiral Sir David Milne who insisted on taking the helm and refused to follow the advice of the ship's master, who knew the waters. As they drifted towards a dangerous shoal, the admiral wanted the captain to resume control, but he was not prepared to be responsible once his authority had been usurped. A dispute followed and it was reported, "A little shipwreck appeared our inevitable fate; however, we dropped into deeper water, & hearing the waves breaking on a shingle beach, the master did let go the anchor." They spent the night there, and next morning sailed safely into Parrsboro Harbour.

During the nineteenth century, Parrsboro was the centre of shipbuilding along this shore, and a port of registry for many locally built schooners and square-rigged ships. The port's facilities attracted commercial shipping, and its importance increased when a railway was opened in 1877 to bring coal from the mines at Springhill for export. Coal carriers, lumber scows, merchant vessels, and fishing boats lined the harbour's wharves.

The four-masted schooner Governor Parr, *launched at the Huntley shipyards in 1919, was the last such schooner built at Parrsboro.*

By the early twentieth century, steamships were beginning to appear in the harbour. Parrsboro's importance as a transhipment port for coal continued until the railway closed in 1958. Today, a few fishing boats and pleasure craft use the harbour, but commercial traffic has left. The wealth of fossils found on the beaches, including the tracks of a tiny dinosaur, attracts visitors to the town and to the Fundy Geological Museum.

The ferry service that originated with the Acadians had many different operators, but during the nineteenth and well into the early twentieth century, there was a daily service from Parrsboro to Kingsport and Wolfville. The last ferry boat, the MV *Kipawo*, ceased operation during the Second World War when she was requisitioned by the Royal Canadian Navy. After many years of service elsewhere, she finally returned to Parrsboro Harbour in the 1980s, to become part of Parrsboro's Ship's Company Theatre building.

There are still a few houses on the Partridge Island shore where the Shannons and the Ratchfords once lived. Ratchford's house was incorporated into Ottawa House by the Sea, later the summer home of Sir Charles Tupper, premier of

Nova Scotia, Father of Confederation, and prime minister of Canada. Ottawa House is now a museum where much of the area's history is preserved.

The road westward leads to Port Greville, with its squat pyramidal lighthouse. This little settlement was one of the many shipbuilding centres along the shore, and its Age of Sail Heritage Museum commemorates the industry that was once so important in the area.

Advocate Harbour

At the entrance to the Minas Channel between the Bay of Fundy and the Minas Basin, there is a harbour and beach that abounds in Mi'kmaw creation legends. It was here at Atuomjek, meaning "the sandy place," that Kluskap is said to have lived in his wigwam. The area is also known as Kluskap's Medicine Garden.

While Champlain was exploring the Bay of Fundy in 1604, he was looking for minerals as required by his mandate from King Henri IV. He came to this harbour where he identified copper deposits (*mines*) but noted that the Fundy tides covered them twice a day. He called the harbour *Port des Mines*, and the name, slightly changed, became attached to the Minas Basin. His map shows the sandy flats in the harbour that are exposed at low tide, and his vessel's anchorage in the channel near the harbour entrance.

A small Acadian farming and fishing settlement grew up here in the late seventeenth century. In 1776, during the American Revolution, Loyalist Luther Morris and his wife arrived. Morris had worked as a weaver, but to survive, he also had to farm and fish. The Morrises were joined by other families and the community grew. The settlers took their catch by boat to Partridge Island, where they traded it for supplies.

In the nineteenth century, many residents made their living from lumbering and merchant shipping. Shipbuilding was established at West Advocate, where the *Windsor* was launched in 1800, followed by several more vessels. The first ship built inside the harbour by one of the Morris family in 1830 was the *Vetruvius*. Altogether, thirty-nine schooners, thirty-two brigantines, and other vessels were built in Advocate shipyards. They provided communications with the outside world, particularly trade with the United States and the West Indies. Shipbuilding ceased in the twentieth century, and steamships sought larger ports, leaving the harbour to the fishing boats.

Residents of Advocate Harbour have always fished, first for survival and later for trade, and a variety of fish are caught and processed here today. Fishing boats draw up beside a protective seawall, but at low tide, they sit high and dry, with just a trickle of water in the channel until the harbour fills again with the incoming tide.

CUMBERLAND BASIN

The coastline of the Cumberland Basin, at the northeastern end of the Bay of Fundy, is shared by New Brunswick and Nova Scotia. In the eighteenth century, when Britain and France were at war, it marked the frontier between New France—French territory—and British-ruled Nova Scotia. Inevitably, it became the scene of confrontations between the rival powers.

The strong tides surging into the basin twice a day deposit huge blocks of red-tinged ice on the shore in winter and spring. They created the salt marshes that attracted the first European settlers to the area. In the late 1600s, some of the Acadians at Port Royal were growing restless. There they lived under constant threat of attack by raiders from New England, and the presence of French officials brought closer supervision of their everyday lives than they had been accustomed to. In 1672, a ship bearing Jacques Bourgeois, his sons, Charles and Germain, and two sons-in-law dropped anchor at the head of the Cumberland Basin, not far from the present town of Amherst, and they began farming here.

Beaubassin and Minudie

The Bourgeois family established the community of Beaubassin on a ridge to the east of the Missaguash River. With other families who joined them, they built dykes to protect against flooding and drained the marsh for cow pasture. Jacques Bourgeois had originally trained as a surgeon, but in Acadie he became a farmer and a shipbuilder. Ships brought supplies, both from France by way of Port Royal, and from Boston merchants, to the little harbour at the mouth of the Missaguash and LaPlanche Rivers. In 1676, Michel LeNeuf de la Vallière received the seigneury of Beaubassin, with land just to the north of the village.

Travel between Beaubassin and Port Royal was easy in summer, but in winter, stormy weather and ice in the rivers and along the shore kept the settlement isolated. In November 1685, LaVallière's ship, delayed by bad weather, barely made it home from Port Royal before the freeze-up. On his return, he found he had an unexpected guest: Jacques de Meulles, Intendant of New France, had made his way across the isthmus from the Northumberland Strait after his ship had run aground off Miscou. He was hoping to continue his journey to Port Royal and was disappointed to wait five months before making sail again. He wrote that he was obliged "in spite of the frosts and the bad weather, to use all of Sieur de LaVallière's dependants to get out of the ice a small ship of 12 tons, which he possessed and which I had to have put in order."

On reaching the harbour mouth, the ship was blown off course and ran aground on a muddy point, where it was quickly stranded by the dropping tide. De Meulles described his experience of the extreme tidal range of the Bay of Fundy as follows: "The two sides of the point seemed like two great ditches three or four fathoms deep, and the bottom of the river was eight fathoms lower than we were, and the sides of the point were very steep." There they had to stay until the tide turned and allowed them to moor in deeper water to await a favourable wind.

Beaubassin was not spared in time of war: in 1696 and 1704, raiders led by Benjamin Church attacked the settlement. Worse was to come because, although Beaubassin was left undisturbed when the British won control of Nova Scotia in 1713, it sat on the disputed border between British and French territory—the Missaguash River. In the lead-up to the Seven Years' War, tension between the two countries increased and British troops, dispatched to Beaubassin in 1750, established Fort Lawrence on the British side of the river. Abbé LeLoutre stirred up the Mi'kmaq, forced the Acadians to cross to Fort Beauséjour on the French side, and burned the village. Fort Beauséjour fell to British troops in 1755 and was renamed Fort Cumberland. This decisive battle was one of the events leading up to Governor Lawrence's order for the deportation of the Acadians. British transport ships carried into exile any former residents of Beaubassin who had not escaped.

Beaubassin was deserted until a contingent of Yorkshire settlers arrived on the *Duke of York* in 1772. More ships followed, and settlements grew up at Amherst and elsewhere around the shore. They were joined by Loyalists and others, and the Chignecto Isthmus became a farming region again. Today, the site of Beaubassin lies under farmland. Archaeologists have found extensive remains of the former community and there is a small interpretive pavilion. The dykes built by the Acadians were maintained by their successors, but they may not be high enough to withstand today's rising water levels, and governments have been urged to raise their level to protect the railway line and the Trans-Canada Highway that run along the Chignecto Isthmus.

Minudie lies off the beaten track, on a peninsula east of the estuary of River Hébert. This was the northern end of the Mi'kmaw route from the Minas Basin. A few Acadian families established farms on the marshlands there that they called *les Champs Élysées*. Those who returned from exile in the 1760s became tenants of Joseph Frederick Wallet DesBarres, whose estate received a portion of the produce from their farms. Some of their descendants were employed by Amos Peck Seaman, a nineteenth-century entrepreneur who was as much concerned with industry as with farming. By 1810, "King" Seaman—as he was called—had established a shipyard with his brother Job on an inlet on the Cumberland Basin at the mouth of Mill Creek, and ships from the little harbour traded with Boston merchants. In 1831, Seaman established a successful grindstone manufacturing business using local sandstone. His vessels carried grindstones to the United States, the West Indies, and elsewhere, returning with stock for his company store.

Seaman died in 1864; his sons predeceased him, and their descendants squabbled among themselves with the result that, by the end of the century, the grindstone business had collapsed. At the same time, wooden vessels were becoming obsolete, so work at the Seaman mill and shipyard also dwindled. Merchant ships ceased to frequent Minudie's harbour, and the area is now almost deserted.

Northumberland Shore

On the north side of the Chignecto Isthmus, we follow an easterly route along the Northumberland Shore through many small settlements. As in other parts of the province, the Mi'kmaq had semi-permanent villages along these shores, going into the shelter of the forest in the winter. In the seventeenth century, Acadian settlers established farms, draining the marshes and clearing some of the forest. After the 1755 Deportation, settlers from New England took over the farms and established sawmilling and shipbuilding communities. Over the years, the economy has changed. Now, in summer and fall, tourists and cottage-owners are drawn to the area for many reasons. They enjoy the beaches, noted for their warm waters, and the quiet beauty of the landscape.

PUGWASH, WALLACE, AND TATAMAGOUCHE HARBOURS

The rivers that empty into the Northumberland Strait form wide shallow harbours. When the Fortress of Louisbourg was established to defend the colony of Île Royale, now known as Cape Breton Island, the Acadian communities on this shore were centres of illicit trade. Produce and cattle were brought from farms on the Minas and Cumberland Basins, and in defiance of British authorities, shipped to feed the soldiers and citizens of Louisbourg.

The ancient Mi'kmaw name of Pawi'kwek, meaning "shallow water," was anglicized by the Planter settlers to Pugwash. A narrow channel at the head of Pugwash Harbour opens into the Pugwash Basin and the sprawling lower reaches of the river. Loyalist refugees joined the community at the time of the American Revolution, and Highland Scots displaced by the Clearances came in the early 1800s. A strong Scottish tradition survives in the community, where there are still street signs in Gaelic.

Vessels line both sides of Pugwash Harbour in 1898.

From the beginning, the people of Pugwash fished for their own use and for trade, and quickly established sawmills and shipyards on the river and harbour. In the nineteenth century, locally built vessels brought prosperity to merchants and provided employment. Lobster canneries and fish-packing plants stood by the shore, and sandstone from a nearby quarry was exported. It was an age of prosperity, and the harbour hummed with activity.

Although the demand for lumber and wooden ships dropped off in the twentieth century, fishing vessels continued to use the harbour. But there were four major fires in the village between 1890 and 1929, and the last one coincided with the beginning of the Great Depression. As the community faced economic disaster, a native of Pugwash, Cyrus Eaton, came to the rescue. Hoping to revive the economy, this wealthy industrialist returned to the village and financed rebuilding after the fire. He improved the harbour facilities for fishing boats with a seawall, and upgraded the community's infrastructure in the hope of making it a tourist destination. He created a park overlooking the harbour and acquired a nearby waterside property which he renovated and opened as an inn. In the 1950s, Eaton decided to host conferences and educational events there. It became Thinkers Lodge, where scientists from both sides of the Iron Curtain met to discuss the dangers of nuclear weapons. From this sprang the Nobel Prize–winning series of Pugwash Conferences on Science and World Affairs.

One of the biggest industrial sites on the south side of Pugwash Harbour is the salt mine. A huge underground salt deposit has been mined since 1959 and the salt is exported from a loading depot on the wharf.

Today, residents are employed mainly in fishing and fish packing. Fisherman's Wharf is a base for the fleet. Lobster is the most valuable catch and is packed for export. Recreational craft tie up at the yacht club, and there is a ramp in town for launching small boats.

The next harbour along this shore is at the mouth of the Wallace River, known for many years by the name of Remsheg, derived from its Mi'kmaw name. The Loyalist community was augmented by Scots who renamed the settlement in honour of both their hero, William Wallace, and Michael Wallace, the provincial treasurer.

Among Wallace's prominent citizens was James Davison, who established a shipyard on the harbour, traded in lumber, and ran a general store. His brother David oversaw the shipyard and sailed to England with cargoes of lumber, returning with goods for the store. Business at the shipyard dropped off at about the time of David's death in 1860, and it closed in 1868.

In the mid-nineteenth century a deposit of sandstone was discovered near Wallace, and quarrying became an important part of the economy. For many years, sandstone was exported from the harbour, but today it is carried out by truck.

Wallace is still an active fishing port, and although a wide variety of fish is harvested, lobster remains the most valuable catch, and is processed at the seafood plant near the wharf.

The next inlet is the bay between the mouths of the French River and Waughs River—the area that the Mi'kmaq named Takumegoochk, "the place where the waters meet." It is close to the shortest sea route between Prince Edward Island and Nova Scotia. When Nicolas Denys passed this way, he observed an abundance of oysters and shellfish.

The Acadians who came here in the early eighteenth century modified the Mi'kmaw name, calling it Tatamagouche. The harbour was the scene of a confrontation when New England troops were besieging Louisbourg in 1745. Four French ships accompanied by a fleet of Mi'kmaw canoes were dispatched from the St. Lawrence to assist in its defence. As they passed through the Northumberland Strait off Tatamagouche Harbour, they encountered a British ship, the *Resolution*. Hoping to avoid attack, the *Resolution*'s captain raised a French flag, pretending to be a French privateer with a prize, but the deception failed and the ship was attacked. After a long fight, the *Resolution* was surrounded by ships and canoes, only to be saved at the last minute by the arrival of two more British vessels. The French and

Mi'kmaq retreated to the shore, where French troops hastily constructed defences to ward off further attacks. A cairn overlooking the harbour commemorates the Battle of Tatamagouche.

In the 1750s many Acadians crossed the strait to Île Saint-Jean (today's Prince Edward Island), which was still held by the French, but some remained at Tatamagouche and were deported with other Acadians in 1755. Their homes were burned, and their farms lay untended until 1765, when Joseph Frederick Wallet DesBarres received a large land grant in the area where he established settlers.

The "French" on French River were not Acadians, but Protestants from Montbéliard who had been brought to Nova Scotia in the early 1750s by DesBarres. They were later joined by Scottish immigrants. Some of these people were farmers, but in the 1800s lumber mills and shipyards became profitable enterprises. Many mills were built on rivers around the bay and Alexander Campbell and two partners established a shipyard on the French River. There were two shipyards on Waughs River, and for much of the nineteenth century, lumber was exported to Britain from this harbour.

Today, one of the major exports is oysters, which along with clams, flourish in the bay. In addition, Tatamagouche Boat Shop demonstrates traditional boat-building skills at Creamery Square. This site is also home to the Arts Centre and the Heritage Centre Museum, all part of the thriving cultural life of the town. Visitors can stay at the unique Train Station Inn, which operates in the restored station, providing accommodation in seven cabooses, and meals in a dining car.

PICTOU HARBOUR

Most visitors to Pictou head to the waterfront to see the brightly painted replica of the ship *Hector*. The nearby interpretive centre tells the story of its passengers, who were some of the area's first immigrants. But the town's history goes back to the days when the Mi'kmaq lived around this large cross-shaped body of water that they called Piktu'k.

Three rivers, known today as the East, Middle, and West Rivers, each with a wide estuary, flow into this harbour, which is protected by a sandbar broken by a narrow channel. This was a traditional meeting point for the Mi'kmaq who travelled along its rivers, and who spent at least part of the year on its shores. There are traces of several encampment sites around the harbour. The Mi'kmaw name is said to mean "an expulsion of gas," perhaps related to the smell of the gas escaping from coal seams in the area, but also associated with human emissions. The Mi'kmaw community of Pictou Landing is on the shores of Pictou and Boat Harbours. In modern times its residents have had to deal with far worse than the smell of gas, as for years the nearby pulp mill has pumped toxic effluent into Boat Harbour, destroying the fishing grounds and threatening people's health. The flow of effluent has now ceased, and the toxic waste is eventually to be removed from Boat Harbour.

When Nicolas Denys wrote about Pictou Harbour in his memoirs, he noted its coves and inlets but did not explore the rivers. The first European immigrants arrived in the 1760s when land was made available to settlers, including a group known as the Philadelphia Company, who acquired acreage in the area now occupied by the town of Pictou. Six families originally from Scotland and Northern Ireland arrived in the harbour on the brig *Betsey* on June 10, 1767. Seeing fires on the shore, they decided to remain aboard overnight in case in case they were attacked as they landed. It turned out that their fears were groundless: some people from Truro had come to meet them and had lit the fires. But meanwhile, John Harris's wife had gone into labour, and their son Thomas was born on the ship. The next morning the passengers disembarked and began the daunting task of clearing land and building homes.

They were followed six years later by the much better known contingent of immigrants aboard the *Hector*, which had come directly from western Scotland. Much celebrated today, the *Hector* was in fact a decrepit old Dutch vessel that was near the end of her days when she set out from Loch Broom in July 1773. She carried nearly two hundred Gaelic-speaking settlers, including a piper whose music kept their spirits up during their long, stormy passage. Provisions had been kept to a minimum and by the time the ship approached Pictou, in mid-September, food supplies had run out, water was rationed, and many passengers were ill.

The immigrants had expected to find farmland waiting for them, but all they saw as they came into the harbour was forest. Nevertheless, they came ashore to the skirl of the bagpipes, which so alarmed a group of curious Mi'kmaq that they took to the woods.

The earlier settlers already occupied much of the land along the shore, so the new arrivals began to clear land along the rivers, building log cabins in which to shelter during the approaching winter. They established subsistence farms, cut lumber, and built ships to carry white pine from Pictou to Britain for masts for the Royal Navy.

When James McGregor arrived in Pictou in 1786 to serve as minister to the settlers, he came overland from Halifax. He was dismayed not to find a town, but rather, a community scattered around the harbour and along the rivers. Among the leading residents was "Squire" Robert Patterson, who had been among the early arrivals on the *Betsey*. MacGregor preached his first sermon in Patterson's barn overlooking the harbour. His audience had come ashore by boat and canoe, apparently in high spirits, which shocked the minster who was used to a more solemn Sabbath demeanour.

Two years later, John "Deacon" Patterson began to develop a site on the north side of the harbour that would become Pictou town. He was an entrepreneur with interests in lumbering and shipbuilding. Alexander and Thomas Copeland and John Dawson also settled in the newly established town and made their living by coastal trading. Other businesses quickly took root, and wharves soon lined the waterfront. Trading schooners took lumber to the West Indies and returned to port with cargoes of sugar, molasses, and rum. The rum was particularly welcomed by the residents—much to the Rev. MacGregor's disapproval—and there were several taverns along the waterfront.

During the American Revolution, some Pictou residents sympathized with the rebels. On one occasion, privateers sailed into the harbour, where a ship, the *Molly*, was loading cargo. Her captain, William Lowden, was lured away by rebel sympathizers and held prisoner while armed raiders seized his ship and sailed her away. When he was freed, Lowden paddled a canoe across the strait to where a British naval vessel was moored in Charlottetown. Alerted, the British sailors set off in pursuit of the *Molly*, recaptured her at Baie Verte along the coast, and brought her safely back to Pictou.

In 1788 a schooner came into the harbour and dropped off a young man who would make a great contribution to Pictou's development. He was a highlander named Edward Mortimer who had come to buy timber on behalf of his employer. He soon set up business for himself and became a successful merchant, trader, and shipbuilder, married Deacon Patterson's daughter, and built a large stone residence overlooking the harbour on what is known as Mortimers Point. He held various public offices and is said to have become the richest man in Nova Scotia. The house was later owned by Lord Strathcona, Chief Factor of the Hudson's Bay Company, who named it Norway House after a company post in the Northwest Territories. Sadly, after several changes of ownership, it suffered from neglect and vandalism and had to be demolished in 2013.

In 1799, the "Big Ship," the *Harriet*, was launched from William Lowden's shipyard. She was the largest vessel to be built in Nova Scotia in the eighteenth century and must have presented a magnificent sight as she sailed from the harbour, captained by Lowden's son, David, bound for England.

Shipping and the lumber trade sustained Pictou's economy, and in the early nineteenth century as many as fifty vessels could be seen in the harbour loading

Pictou (from Norway House), engraved by W. H. Lizars, ca. 1841. Norway House was built by Edward Mortimer. The view across the harbour shows the wharves and warehouses along the waterfront.

square timber. Ships brought back goods from distant ports, and prosperous entrepreneurs built the fine stone houses that still stand in the town.

Local boat captains could navigate the harbour's narrow entrance, but pilots were constantly in demand to guide large vessels safely into port. Further safeguard was provided by a lighthouse at the end of the sandbar, which became known as Lighthouse Beach. The last of a series of lighthouses burned in 2004.

A fortunate circumstance in 1803 gave Pictou its foremost educator. The Rev. Dr. Thomas McCulloch, his wife, and three children were on their way to Prince Edward Island, where McCulloch was to serve as minister. The ship on which they were travelling put into Pictou Harbour in November and the family disembarked, planning to cross to the Island. But it was late in the season, and the local people advised against trying to cross the strait because of the weather. The family spent the winter in Pictou, where the townspeople persuaded McCulloch to remain and serve as minister in the town's Harbour Church. Soon after taking up his appointment he began a school for boys in his house, which developed into the prestigious Pictou Academy.

Many tradesmen came to work in Pictou, including a well-known manufacturer of spinning wheels, named MacIntosh. Roland H. Sherwood recounts, in his book entitled *Pictou's Past*, a tale of disaster in the harbour in the early days of the nineteenth century. At that time, women in rural Nova Scotia spun their own wool and flax for weaving into cloth. It seems that in 1815 a Trenton woman bought a spinning wheel from MacIntosh in exchange for a bag of barley flour to be delivered the following year. The woman carried the wheel on her back over the harbour ice and up the East River. Next spring, she and seven relatives set out in a boat with the bag of flour to pay MacIntosh. The boat capsized in the harbour, all her relatives were drowned, and the flour was lost, but the woman somehow survived. It is said that MacIntosh never claimed his payment.

Shipbuilding suffered a setback at the end of the nineteenth century, but Pictou had another valuable resource. In 1798 James MacGregor had discovered coal on his property on the East River. In 1807 his neighbour, John MacKay, obtained an export licence, and coal was shipped from Pictou Harbour soon afterwards. The mineral rights were later acquired by the General Mining Company, which started exporting coal in 1827. This was the beginning of major industrial development in the area around New Glasgow. In 1830 a locally built steamship, the *Richard Grant*, began towing coal carriers down to the harbour, and other steam-powered tugboats followed. The railway came to Pictou in 1867, bringing coal from the mine to Pictou Landing for transfer to ships. Passengers for Pictou town also disembarked here and travelled across the harbour by a steam ferry, the *Mayflower*.

Steamships were increasingly seen in the harbour as the nineteenth century progressed. In 1833, the SS *Royal William* called here before making her historic journey to England and back, said to be the first transatlantic voyage powered entirely by steam. Besides merchant shipping and ferries to Pictou Landing and New Glasgow, steamers ran regularly between Pictou and Charlottetown, the Magdalen Islands, and Montreal.

From early days, fish had helped sustain the settlers, and an important commercial fishery developed in the Northumberland Strait. The first Pictou Lobster Carnival was held in 1934; it has grown into an annual three-day event with a wide range of popular activities.

In 1939, when King George VI and Queen Elizabeth visited Canada, crowds watched as a Canadian cruiser brought the royal couple into Pictou Harbour. This was just a few weeks before the Second World War broke out, an event that brought changes to Pictou. The Pictou Foundry and the Ferguson Shipyard were expanded in 1942, with new wharves built by the Foundation Maritime Company, providing deeper berths for freighters that were hastily built to carry supplies across the Atlantic to help the war effort. When the hostilities ended, the Ferguson yards

Government Wharf, Pictou, in 1948, with railcars and vessels. During the Second World War, corvettes were refitted at the adjacent outfitting wharf.

continued to construct ships in Pictou until 1984, by which time they had built another 107 vessels of various kinds. Since then, the Pictou Shipyard has continued to operate under different owners, specializing in repairs.

A major attraction for many years was the building of the replica of the *Hector* at the Heritage Quay on Pictou's waterfront, beginning in the 1990s. She was launched in September 2000 and is open to the public in summer. An interpretive centre allows visitors to imagine the experience of the early settlers who arrived in the harbour with their piper after the long Atlantic crossing.

The heavy industries that developed during the nineteenth century in Pictou's hinterland all went into decline during the next century. Meanwhile, a pulp mill was established at Abercrombie Point, between the East and Middle Rivers, which brought steady employment into the community. It also became the source of complaints, as toxic residue from the plant was pumped into Boat Harbour, and fumes from the plant drifted over the town of Pictou. The Mi'kmaw community of Pictou Landing has suffered the most from this pollution, in many ways, both from loss of livelihood and from related sicknesses.

After more than thirty years of toxic pollution and endless promises to clean up Boat Harbour, and with several changes in the mill's ownership, legislation brought about the shutdown of the mill in early 2020, resulting in the loss of many jobs. In order to resume operations, the mill will have to meet strict environmental standards.

ST. GEORGES BAY

The road continues eastward from Pictou to the shallow, sandy harbours around St. Georges Bay. They are interesting communities for their ethnic diversity and mixture of cultures. Antigonish has strong Scottish and Irish connections, while eastward are several predominantly Acadian villages. As well, there are long-established Mi'kmaw and Black communities. The people who originally settled here worked mainly on farms and in the forests, but there were also people who fished in the shallow waters of St. Georges Bay.

Antigonish and Pomquet

Although Antigonish Harbour is the largest of the inlets between Cape St. George and the Strait of Canso, it is the least accessible for shipping. As at Pictou, there is a narrow channel through a long sandbar at the entrance to the harbour, which is at the confluence of two rivers—the West and South Rivers—separated by Williams Point.

Navigable by canoe and rich in wildlife, the area was home to Mi'kmaw communities. Its name was Nalegitkoonecht, sometimes interpreted as "where branches are torn off." When Nicolas Denys explored the coast in the seventeenth century, he was impressed with the expanse of sand exposed in the area at low tide and the abundance of shellfish which the Mi'kmaq harvested there. Denys noted that visiting French fishing fleets had established a fur trade.

The first permanent European settlers on the harbour were Scots, arriving in the 1770s; they were later joined by more of their countrymen. Then came a group of Irish Loyalists, led by Captain Timothy Hierlihy, who received a grant of land after the American Revolution which included the present town site. It was originally named Dorchester, but quickly reverted to a form of the Mi'kmaw name, Antigonish.

Hierlihy and his followers welcomed Lord Dalhousie, the lieutenant governor, when he visited Antigonish in September 1817. The town and harbour narrowly escaped yet another name change when a delegation of residents asked His Honour's consent to honour him by adopting his name. He sensibly refused, saying that changing the name by which the harbour was known on all maps and charts would cause too much confusion.

Antigonish developed quickly during the nineteenth century to become the commercial and administrative centre for the area, but because the harbour was silted up, goods could not be brought in or exported at a town wharf. The nearest navigable water was a mile away. When Joseph Howe visited in 1831, he observed that "produce must be sent that distance by land, and then carried in boats, before it is shipped for transportation by sea." He described the state of the head of the harbour, where "old stumps, driftwood, and sunken stones were scattered about in most admired disorder." A proposal to clear and deepen a channel to the town was passed by the House of Assembly but voted down by the Council until a member of that body visited the site, saw its condition, and persuaded his colleagues to fund the project.

In the early twentieth century a coastal packet service ran from the public wharf at Antigonish Landing to communities on St. Georges Bay, and small trading schooners still came to the Landing. The idea of installing a permanent structure to maintain a deep passage through the sandbar was discarded because of cost. Further recommendations were made for dredging a channel into the harbour, in order to export gypsum and forest products from the surrounding area. An engineer, Andrew MacGillivray, observed in a 1925 report that "with the exception of fishing and pleasure boats, very few craft visit the harbour" and he recommended regular dredging to facilitate commercial shipping of pulpwood, which was a major product of this region. Dredging was carried out in 1927, and ships laden with pulpwood continued to leave the harbour for some years, but Antigonish never became a major harbour.

Today, the town is a lively cultural centre with a university, theatre, annual Highland Games, and local history museum in the former train station. There is a wildlife sanctuary at the head of the harbour, and a scenic trail leads along the water to Antigonish Landing.

Pomquet Harbour is the first of the settlements established by Acadians to the east of Antigonish. The Mi'kmaq named the area Pogumkek (spellings vary). In the eighteenth century it was home to twenty-three Mi'kmaw families. Today, the Paq'tnkek First Nation Reserve near Afton also has two parcels of this traditional land on Pomquet Harbour.

Five Acadian families who had returned from exile in St. Malo, France, came here in 1773, and received grants on the harbour in 1798. They were joined by other returning Acadians and more settlers, mostly French speaking, who came in the nineteenth century. Life was hard at first, but they made their living by fishing, farming, and cutting lumber from the forest. Many of their descendants still live in Pomquet. The area has retained its language and culture, and today, Acadian children are educated in French.

Tracadie

Tracadie was known to the Mi'kmaq as Telakatik, meaning "camping place"—their traditional summer fishing ground. Like other harbours on St. Georges Bay, it is shallow, and protected by a sandbar. The land around it was settled in the 1770s by Pierre Benoit and the Fougère brothers, who had worked at the fishing community of Arichat. Others joined them in the 1780s.

Among these settlers was Jean-Joseph Gerroir, one of the Acadians who had avoided exile by overcoming the crew of the ship on which they were being deported. They all escaped and fled to Memramcook. Jean-Joseph was caught and imprisoned in Halifax. On his release he made his way to Chezzetcook and eventually to Tracadie, where his son, sea captain Joseph Gerroir, later became a community leader. The Gerroirs farmed a large acreage on Tracadie Harbour.

The end of the American Revolution brought Scottish and Irish Loyalist settlers to the harbour, and a group of Black Loyalists were given land farther up the Tracadie River. By the nineteenth century, farming, fishing, and lumbering were the mainstays, and these continued through the twentieth century.

In the 1820s a Trappist Monastery was founded in Tracadie, where the monks ran a farm, gristmill, and carding mill on their property at the head of the harbour. They were also in close contact with the Mi'kmaq in the area. The monastery buildings were twice destroyed by fire, and the few remaining monks moved away. Their presence is commemorated by the name of the community of Monastery at the former site.

Havre Boucher

The most easterly settlement on St. Georges Bay is Havre Boucher. According to Archbishop Plessis's diary, the community takes its name from a Captain François Boucher from Quebec, who is said to have sheltered there in a storm in the winter of 1759 and remained there until spring. An alternative explanation is that the name was originally Havre Bouché, meaning "blocked harbour," from the sandspit at the harbour entrance.

The original residents were Acadians who had spent their exile in Arichat and Saint-Malo. The local population was increased by some Highland Scots, who had arrived in Pictou in 1791 and moved eastwards, and Irish immigrants who came in the early nineteenth century. Most of the residents of Havre Boucher, whatever their origin, launched small fishing boats in the harbour in order to harvest lobster and scallops.

A Catholic priest, Father Vincent de Paul recorded:

So recently as the month of August, 1823, I was in a parish called Havre-à-Bouchers, when twenty-six canoes filled with Indians arrived there; they came to have their children baptized, and for confession, &c. There were eight singers among them, and during the week that they remained, they sang mass for me each day, and one might say conducted themselves like canons or like Trappists! They have clear voices.

By 1878 Havre Boucher was a thriving community, home to ships' captains, merchants, and fishers. It suffered a decline in the twentieth century, and some people found work elsewhere. But today, fishing boats still leave from the wharf near the harbour entrance.

Although these three villages maintain a strong Acadian component, the population includes many newcomers, including residents who commute to Antigonish or Port Hawkesbury or even further afield. The greatest activity in the harbours today takes place in May and June, when it is lobster season in St. Georges Bay.

Cape Breton Island

Like many islands around the world, Cape Breton has its own distinctive culture that is a source of pride to its people. The region has a special place in the hearts of those who were born there, no matter where they may be across Canada or abroad. In the past, French, Scots, and people from around the world sought refuge and built new lives around its harbours. Today, these places are renowned for music, scenery, and hospitality, and draw Cape Bretoners home.

Cape Breton—initially referring to a point of land on the Atlantic coast rather than the whole island—takes its name from the seasonal fishing fleets that came from Brittany, and it begins to appear on maps of early explorations in the sixteenth century. The island's scenic Cabot Trail is named for explorer John Cabot, who is believed to have made landfall on the shore of Aspy Bay in 1497, before Europeans came to other parts of Nova Scotia. He is commemorated there by Cabots Landing Historic Site and Provincial Park.

The Mi'kmaq named the island Unama'ki, meaning "land of the fog." They welcomed the Spanish, Portuguese, or French cod fishers working the offshore banks who came into the harbours every summer to process their catch. In the 1620s, the British king, Charles I, granted Sir William Alexander the right to establish the colony of New Scotland, or Nova Scotia, which included the island of Cape Breton. When the region was ceded to France by treaty in 1632, the island became part of Acadie, and was given the name Île Royale. Mainland Nova Scotia became permanently British in 1713, but the island remained in French hands for another half-century.

After the fall of Quebec, the French empire in North America collapsed, and in 1763 the island officially became part of Nova Scotia. The British government was in no hurry to populate it until 1784, when an influx of Loyalists sailed into Sydney Harbour to take up land grants and, for a short time, Cape Breton became a separate colony. Its status was revoked in 1820, and it rejoined Nova Scotia.

HARBOURS ON THE STRAIT OF CANSO

The Strait of Canso is just one kilometre wide at its narrowest point, so for the Mi'kmaq in their high-sided sea canoes, and for settlers in small boats, crossing to the mainland was not difficult. For much of the nineteenth century, private ferry services carried passengers to and from the fishing harbours of Point Tupper, Port Hawkesbury, and Plaster Cove (later Port Hastings). The ferryman towed a barge behind his boat to carry a horse and wagon.

With the establishment of railways on both sides of the strait in the 1890s, at first, a barge carried just two railcars at a time between Mulgrave and Point Tupper. A more efficient rail ferry was in place by the time the Canso Causeway was opened in 1955. The causeway had both a road for cars and trucks and a railway line, and the train ferry was retired. This resulted in a loss of business for Point Tupper, but its deepwater port facilities attracted cargo vessels, and more recently it became home to a bulk coal terminal.

A car ferry ran between Mulgrave and Port Hawkesbury from 1902 until the causeway was opened. Now, after crossing the causeway by road, travellers arrive in Port Hastings, where the Visitor Information Centre and museum introduces them to Cape Breton culture and history. Port Hawkesbury no longer hosts a ferry service, but it is a busy commercial seaport, shipping crushed rock and gravel from the area, and handling trans-shipments of petroleum.

SYDNEY HARBOUR

In early days, most travellers to Île Royale had their first glimpse of its landscape as they sailed through Spanish Bay into Sydney Harbour. In the twenty-first century, many people still enter Sydney Harbour either on a cruise ship or on a ferry from Newfoundland.

The old names of Baie des Espagnols or Spanish Bay remind us that the first visitors "from away" were Spanish fishers, who used the harbour as shelter for their boats and cargoes of fish. There they met the Mi'kmaq, who had been living for thousands of years on the harbour. They welcomed the visitors with whom they traded furs for tools and other implements. When the spread of European settlement impinged on the Mi'kmaw way of life, there was discontent. The colonial government established a reserve on the shore, but in 1916 the community was forced to move to the present site of the Membertou Reserve. Here, the Mi'kmaq have established successful businesses, but they have not relinquished their claim to their traditional lands around the harbour.

In the eighteenth century, the harbour became a place of many arrivals and departures. In the 1740s a group of Acadians who felt threatened in Nova Scotia set sail for Île Royale. Some of them formed a small settlement at the head of the bay. The French controlled the area from their fortress at Louisbourg, and from time to time officers from the garrison visited the Acadian settlements.

It may have been on such a visit that Jules-César Félix de la Noue met Marguerite Guédry, whose family had come from Merligueche. They fell in love, but la Noue's superior officer forbade their marriage on the grounds that Marguerite's grandmother was Mi'kmaw, and officers were not allowed to marry Indigenous women. Nevertheless, a priest from Port Dauphin (present-day St. Anns) agreed to marry them. When the authorities found out about the marriage, it was declared "clandestine, scandalous, and abusive," and was promptly annulled. Jules-César was thrown into jail and he and the priest were sent back to France. Marguerite and her family packed up and sailed away in disgrace.

That same year, most of the Acadians living around the harbour, discouraged by the poor farming conditions, and perhaps resenting the officious supervision exercised by the French officials in Louisbourg, also embarked with their possessions and returned to the mainland.

Following the final fall of Louisbourg in 1758, colonial authorities began to develop the area's coal deposits on the north shore of the harbour. When American privateers attempted raids on the harbour during the Revolution, Major Timothy Herlihy's troops on board HMS *Hope* fought back and won. The American prisoners were put to work in the coal mines. By 1788 a mine and a coal wharf were operating on the harbour, but the British were slow to develop the resource on a large scale so as not to compete with mines in England which were exporting coal to the colonies.

When the colony of Cape Breton was established to receive Loyalists, the new lieutenant governor, Joseph Frederick Wallet DesBarres, selected the South Arm of the harbour as the site for its capital. The town was named Sydney, in honour of British parliamentarian Thomas Townsend, 1st Viscount Sydney, who was responsible for DesBarres's appointment. In November 1784, a group of disbanded soldiers and impoverished English citizens who were recruited by DesBarres arrived on the *Blenheim*, hoping to build new lives, followed by Loyalists who were sponsored and provided with supplies by the British government. Two months later, DesBarres's ship brought him to Sydney to take up his appointment.

Sydney's early days were not easy. There were disputes among the colonists, and DesBarres fell out with Lord Sydney over his attempt to establish a whale fishery, and over his unauthorized expenditures. In 1786 he was recalled to Britain

The harbour ferry waits at the Cape Breton Electrical Company's ferry terminal at North Sydney, ca. 1900.

to explain matters, and the following year he sailed out of the harbour for the last time, leaving it to his successors to oversee the establishment of the settlement.

In the early nineteenth century, Scottish immigrants who had been displaced by the Highland Clearances began to come to Cape Breton. As they came into Sydney Harbour after their long voyage, they saw the distant mountains that reminded them of home and perhaps gave them hope as they began the hard task of starting a new life.

During the nineteenth and early twentieth centuries, immigrants came into the harbour from all over the world seeking employment. Some worked in the nearby coal mines, and when Sydney's steel plant opened in 1901, many came to form the ethnically diverse community of Whitney Pier. Some operated coal carriers and vessels bringing iron ore from Newfoundland. Others crewed merchant vessels that left from the harbour's wharves and returned with goods for the local consumers. Skilled workmen came to North Sydney's shipyard, and many others found work on fishing boats and in the fish-processing plants.

North Sydney became a major commercial port, but one unfortunate vessel never got far from the harbour. In 1851, the largest wooden ship ever built in Cape Breton—the *Lord Clarendon*—was launched at North Sydney. A huge, square-rigged vessel, she sailed away with a cargo of lumber, but soon ran into a severe storm and returned to North Sydney for repairs. Luck was not with her: on a second attempt to leave, she ran aground in another storm at Low Point, in the harbour entrance, where a lighthouse had stood since 1832. She did not sustain much damage initially and could perhaps have been refloated, but the weather worsened and two of her masts were carried away. The crew was rescued, along with some of her cargo, but the ship broke up and was lost.

As settlements began to take root, communication across the harbour was provided by a ferry, operated by private boat owners from North Sydney, in the late 1850s. This service was later taken up by the Cape Breton Electrical Company.

By 1870, North Sydney was Canada's fourth largest seaport, with ships carrying goods and passengers in and out of the harbour. In 1898, a ferry service was initiated between North Sydney and Port aux Basques in Newfoundland. The first ferry boat was the SS *Bruce*, operated by the Reid Newfoundland Railway Company. She arrived in Sydney Harbour from Port aux Basques on July 1, beginning a service that is now operated by Marine Atlantic. A second ferry operates in summer providing service to Argentia, Newfoundland.

Sydney Harbour played a vital role in both world wars when it became a naval base, similar to Halifax, where convoys of ships and escort vessels formed to take supplies to Britain. For many of the sailors and merchant seamen, this would be their first, and possibly only sight of Cape Breton, and the last time they would set foot on land before embarking on a dangerous journey across the Atlantic.

It was not only convoys that were attacked. On October 13, 1942, during the Second World War, tragedy came to North Sydney. The ferry SS *Caribou* left harbour that day for Newfoundland with 237 passengers on board. She encountered a German U-boat in the Gulf of St. Lawrence and was torpedoed. There were 101 survivors.

The steel mill and the coal mines were closed at the beginning of the twenty-first century, and ore and coal carriers no longer use the harbour. During its years of operation, the mill's coke ovens had dumped large quantities of toxic waste in what were known as the Tar Ponds, and the harbour itself was polluted. The cleanup of the Tar Ponds, and the creation of a park in their place, resulted in great improvements to both the former industrial area and the harbour. Harbour dredging completed in 2012 enables seasonal cruise ships to come to Sydney's Marine Terminal, and a boardwalk and a marina on the waterfront have made this section of Cape Breton's busiest harbour a pleasant recreational area.

Swordfishing Boats at Glace Bay, ca. 1948. The swordfish fishing industry was a major source of income in the 1940s.

GLACE BAY AND MORIEN BAY

The road eastward from Sydney passes through the mining area of the Cape Breton coalfield. Overlooking the waters of Glace Bay, the Miners' Museum, with its pithead machinery, tells the story of an industry that, for centuries, was the heartbeat of the communities on this part of the coast.

In the early eighteenth century, Baye de Morienne (Morien Bay) was the nearest source of coal to the Fortress of Louisbourg. Coal seams could be easily seen in the cliffs and in surface outcrops, and could be mined directly from the cliffs or from shallow pits. By 1724, ships were carrying fuel to the fortress, and coal was also being shipped to Boston—the beginning of Canada's commercial coal industry. A French mine at Cap-la-Table (Table Head at Glace Bay) also supplied coal to the fortress.

Although coal was shipped along the coast, the French authorities did not allow it to be carried overseas. This may have been to protect French mining companies, or it may have been for safety reasons, as coal from this area gives off a gas that can cause spontaneous combustion, presenting a danger to vessels on a long voyage.

When the British took control of the region, they were slow to develop the coal reserves. A 1760 map identifies scattered coal outcrops all along the shores of the bays, but the only one being officially developed at that time was a "Coal Mine Workt at Present for the King" with its wharf on the shore of Morien Bay, also known as Cow Bay. A settlement was beginning to develop there, and by 1800, Morien had become a busy company town with hundreds of miners.

Glace Bay grew in importance after large-scale underground mining began in 1861, at the Hub Shaft. The mining community grew up in the area near Table Head and within a few years twelve mines were working there, operated by several private companies. In 1894, the Dominion Coal Company was granted exclusive coal mining rights in Cape Breton and it continued to develop the industry. Glace Bay Harbour was busy with coal carriers for many years, until the company built a rail line to carry the coal to the larger ports of Louisbourg and Sydney in the early twentieth century. By the end of the century the mines had closed as markets for Cape Breton coal had collapsed.

Fishing was another major industry in Glace Bay and Morien, but it suffered seriously when the cod fishery collapsed in the 1990s. Swordfish, which had been a commercial catch in the 1930s and had flourished through the 1940s, dwindled in the mid-twentieth century. The fishery struggled though some lean years, but today it brings in a variety of fish for processing and packing. As in other areas, the lobster season is the busiest and most lucrative.

Louisbourg

The harbour at Louisbourg was to France what Halifax was to England in the long years of struggle for colonial rule of eastern North America. Visitors to Louisbourg today find themselves transported back in time to the streets of an eighteenth-century fortified town overlooking the harbour which, for a time, was filled with French naval vessels, fishing boats, and trading ships. Today, costumed interpreters represent merchants, tradesmen, and tavern keepers; women tend the gardens and domestic animals, while soldiers guard the gates and march through the streets. The town is protected by stone walls, with gates on the harbour side and high bastions facing inland. This is a reconstruction of Louisbourg as it was in the early 1740s, before the first siege by the British.

At the beginning of the eighteenth century, Havre-à-l'Anglois on the east side of Cape Breton island had been used by English fishing boats, but came under French jurisdiction with the Treaty of Utrecht, when mainland Nova Scotia was awarded to the British, and the sparsely populated Île Royale given to the French.

In 1714, several French settlers and soldiers, including military engineer Jacques L'Hermitte, were brought to Havre-à-l'Anglois to establish a fortified fishing base, originally to be named Port Saint-Louis. They brought fishing boats and gear, six cannons and ammunition, horse, mules, food, and other supplies for what would become France's chief Atlantic outpost and the centre of its lucrative cod fishery. It was also strategically placed to defend the entrance of the St. Lawrence River and the route to Quebec.

Military surveyors were dispatched to other parts of the island to select the best site for a major fortification, and maps and plans of various harbour sites went back to France with their findings and recommendations. All decisions were made in Paris, and ultimately Port Saint-Louis was chosen as the location for the most ambitious project yet to be undertaken by the French on the Atlantic coast. Once the selection had been confirmed, a succession of French engineers set to work to enlarge the settlement on Rochefort Point, at the south side of the harbour entrance.

A project of this kind could not be completed overnight, but gradually the buildings of the town and the great bastions that were to defend the landward approach rose up on the south side of harbour. Because the engineers were meticulous in recording the stages of construction and sending their plans back to France, there is an excellent record of the work of transforming the fishing village to the garrison town that would be known as Louisbourg. The haphazardly placed fish huts along the shore were replaced by a walled town with an orderly layout of streets. It was not only a major fortification, it was also the commercial and administrative capital of Île Royale. Joseph Monbeton de Brouillon, otherwise known as Saint-Ovide, was appointed governor.

Soldiers' barracks, officers' quarters, and the governor's residence were built to accommodate the growing population. There were stores and warehouses, fish processing facilities, hotels and taverns, and residences. Fishing stages lined the shore outside the town's walls. While the military men all came from France, the town was also populated with fishers, artisans and traders, shopkeepers, and tavernkeepers, some of whom were Acadians, some from France, and others from fishing villages in Newfoundland. There were also surgeons and apothecaries, clergy and nuns, domestic servants and a few slaves brought by government officials, military officers, or merchants.

Even in times of peace, piracy was rife in the seas off Cape Breton. In 1721, the number of troops in the garrison increased and defences were constructed all around the harbour. Gun batteries were built at strategic sites on each side of the harbour entrance, on Battery Island in the harbour mouth, and on the shore on each side of the town. The Grand or Royal Battery stood directly facing the harbour entrance.

Well protected, Louisbourg Harbour quickly became one the most important fishing ports in New France. The wharves and fish stages lay beyond the main landward entrance to the walled town, where the Dauphin Gate, with its impressive towers and archway, controlled access across the moat. There was also an entrance through a more modest archway leading directly from the beach, where boats could be drawn up. A small fishing settlement grew up at the Northeast Harbour.

Shipwrecks were all too frequent along this coast, and in August 1725, word came that a large ship had broken up on the rocks at nearby Baleine. Officers set out from Louisbourg and found the wreckage of the king's ship *Chameau*. Her cargo and passengers, including the newly appointed Intendant of Quebec, were lost. Between two hundred and three hundred people are estimated to have lost their lives, and one hundred and eighty bodies were washed ashore and buried in a mass grave by the priest at Baleine. The shoreline, the weather, and the ocean currents were significant hazards to shipping. Eventually, in 1734, the first lighthouse in what is now Canada was built on a point at the northern entrance to Louisbourg Harbour.

Fishing and trading vessels brought a lot of merchant activity to the town, as ships from ports in Europe, Quebec, New England, and the West Indies delivered and took on cargo. Cattle and produce were imported from farms on the mainland. The French navy transported officials from France and Quebec, as well as troops to man the defences. The harbour was a training base for the navy and it was also a haven for French pirates who attacked English merchant vessels in the North Atlantic.

In winter, all this activity dropped off, as navigation was dangerous and ice frequently blocked the harbour entrance. Provisions would begin running low towards spring and there were many reasons for discontent. Louisbourg was an unpopular posting for the troops; communication with France was sometimes delayed so that soldiers waited for months for their pay, and they were often demoralized and unwilling to obey orders.

Such was the state of affairs in 1745, when France and Britain were once more at war, and a large British naval force, consisting mainly of New Englanders, was sailing towards Louisbourg. Unaware of their approach, the governor was holding a ball, perhaps hoping to bring some levity and merriment after a long chilling winter. The festivities were interrupted when Antoine de la Boularderie and some concerned companions burst into the governor's quarters and raised the alarm.

Louisbourg's swordfish fleet in the harbour in 1935. Swordfish was a valuable catch in the 1930s and '40s.

Following an initial blockade of the harbour, troops landed on Gabarus Bay on May 11 and approached Louisbourg from the rear, seizing the Grand Battery and laying siege to the fortress. They established positions around the harbour from which they attacked the Island Battery and the town. The French forces were unable to repel the attackers, and after a long siege, Governor Louis de Chambon surrendered on June 28, 1745.

Most of the residents of Louisbourg boarded ships that would take them back to France, leaving British troops to occupy the town and control its harbour. The French still had ambitions to regain the fortress, but a doomed expedition led by the duc d'Anville in 1746 got no further than Halifax. Luck was with the French in 1748 when Louisbourg was returned to them with the Treaty of Aix-la-Chapelle that brought the war to an end. Within a year, many of the exiles had returned to their homes and businesses and the harbour was busy again.

Peace did not last for long. In 1754, Augustin Boschenry de Drucour sailed into Louisbourg Harbour to serve as the last governor of Île Royale. The Seven Years' War between European powers pitted Britain and France against each other once more in 1756. The following year British ships again sailed for Louisbourg. French naval vessels repelled the attack, but by 1758, many of the French ships had been deployed to fight elsewhere, leaving only eleven vessels in the harbour to defend the fortress. With the threat of another attack, five of those ships were sunk to block the harbour entrance. Another was seized by two British vessels as it tried to slip away in the fog. The remaining five had transferred much of their manpower and weaponry to the fortress.

The British Navy arrived on June 2, 1758, with an overwhelming force of one hundred and fifty transports, forty men-of-war, and nearly fourteen thousand troops under the command of Geoffrey Amherst. The fleet again anchored in Gabarus Bay and, after waiting out a spell of bad weather, attempted a landing on June 8. They were initially repelled, but a contingent led by James Wolfe established a beachhead and led the landing. Once again British troops besieged the fortress, seizing the lighthouse area, and establishing batteries around the harbour. The final attack began on June 19.

Over the next few days, the walls of the fortress began to give way under cannon and mortar fire. One French ship caught fire and the flames spread to two more. Another shot ignited the King's Bastion two days later. On June 25, under cover of the fog, a British party set fire to one of the two remaining French ships and captured the other. The French surrendered the following day. This was the beginning of the end for French control of territories in Canada. Louisbourg Harbour was the base from which Wolfe attacked and seized Quebec in 1759, and following the surrender of Montreal in 1760, British troops demolished the fortress.

After the dust had settled, it was some time before the harbour of Louisbourg resumed its former character as a fishing port. A small fishing village slowly grew up across the harbour from the fortress site, augmented by some Loyalist settlers in the 1780s. When the vessel on which Lieutenant Governor Dalhousie was travelling moored in the harbour in 1818, his impression was of a "miserable & deserted village." But the village was less deserted than he thought, and fishing families continued to live well during the nineteenth century.

A new lighthouse was built in 1842, close to the remains of the old one, making the harbour safer for fishing and merchant vessels. In 1895, a loading pier and a freight wharf were built, and a railway brought coal from Cape Breton's mines to a fleet of coal carriers.

During the Second World War, the harbour was fortified for use by the Canadian navy for times when Sydney Harbour was blocked by ice. Naval vessels anchored there and onshore facilities for their crews were provided by the community's Navy League branch. In January 1943, an ice-covered American submarine chaser ran aground on the bar at the harbour entrance. After several attempts by local people with fishing boats, the crew was rescued. The men were brought to shore suffering from exposure and were cared for by the local community.

After the war, fishing boats, merchant vessels, and coal carriers continued to use the harbour, but the ups and downs of the coal industry and the fishery brought uncertainty, and by the 1960s, both were in decline. At this time the area received a major boost when Parks Canada began reconstruction of a section of the eighteenth-century town, as part of its development as a National Historic Site.

Today, the reconstructed fortress is a tourist destination, and it is sometimes visited by small cruise ships which anchor in the harbour. Fishing boats still bring their catch to the wharf on the north shore, to be processed in the nearby seafood plant. Louisbourg is a lively place in summer, but in winter it reverts to its original character as a quiet fishing village.

ST. PETERS BAY

South of the Bras d'Or Lake, the road runs across a narrow strip of land between the lake and St. Peters Bay, with a swing bridge over the St. Peters Canal. The nearby Nicolas Denys Museum is locally operated, and the canal, with traces of Denys's fort nearby, is managed by Parks Canada. Battery Provincial Park includes the site of later forts and offers walkers and campers spectacular views of the historic harbour.

From prehistoric times, the Mi'kmaq carried canoes over the short portage route between the bay and the lake. The first foreign fishing boats coming to this harbour were Portuguese, and the sailors called it San Pedro. They were followed in the seventeenth century by French crews from La Rochelle who changed the name to Saint-Pierre. They arrived with supplies for the summer and with merchandise they could trade with the Mi'kmaq. They returned with a cargo of cod and furs. Nicolas Denys established a year-round fishing settlement in 1650 with a fort and dwellings at the head of the bay. He developed the Mi'kmaw portage route as a haul-over, where boats could be skidded across from the harbour to St. Peters Inlet on the Bras d'Or Lake. He later wrote that Saint-Pierre had disadvantages as a harbour because large vessels could not come close to land but had to anchor offshore. Smaller boats brought the catch in to be processed at the settlement but, Denys cautioned, "It is necessary to be well acquainted with the channel, which winds about; and besides there is a quantity of rocks which are not visible."

In 1653, Saint-Pierre was raided by men working for a rival French merchant, and Denys was taken prisoner. He later returned, and continued fishing and trading until the winter of 1668–1669, when a disastrous fire that began in the granary destroyed "merchandise, furniture, ammunition, provisions, flour, wine, arms; in brief, everything." Denys and his men escaped in their nightshirts and were able to save only half a cask each of wine and brandy, and enough wheat to see them through the winter, after which they abandoned the settlement.

The bay came to life again in 1713 when the French were fortifying Île Royale, and it was renamed Port Toulouse. Denys's haul-over was used to ship supplies for Louisbourg through the Bras d'Or Lake. Fort Toulouse was built on Pointe Jérôme, now part of the provincial park, to guard the supply route. As well as the garrison, some sixty Acadian families settled in a new fishing village at Grande Grave Harbour, on the east side of the bay, where the fishing boats brought their catch to dry on the *grave* (from *grève*, meaning "beach").

As the wars continued between France and Britain, the Mi'kmaq continued to support the French cause, and band chiefs came to Port Toulouse from both Cape Breton and the mainland every year to renew their alliance in a solemn ceremony. In early May 1745, the French, Acadians, and Mi'kmaq repelled British raiders, only to see the enemy return with a larger force, burn down the fort and the settlement, before sailing on to capture Louisbourg.

When Île Royale was restored to France after the war, the Acadians who had left Saint-Pierre returned to rebuild their homes and resume their fishing, but after Louisbourg fell for the last time, they were deported.

In 1793, during the French Revolution, there was again a military presence in the community. British soldiers built Fort Dorchester at the top of Mount Granville, guarding both the harbour approaches and the lake.

The present village of St. Peters was established in the early 1800s. The old haulage road was revived, and small sailing vessels could be dragged by oxen from the harbour to the inland sea. The nineteenth century was a time of rapid development, and in 1825, plans were initiated to replace the haul-over with a canal. St. Peters Canal was opened in 1869, with a lock to accommodate the difference in water level between the harbour and the lake. For the first time, small commercial vessels could sail directly between the Atlantic Ocean and the Bras d'Or Lake to reach the rapidly developing industrial area around Sydney, avoiding the long and risky journey around the coast. This route was particularly valuable for transporting coal during both world wars when U-boats threatened coastal shipping. Commercial vessels used the canal well into the twentieth century, but since the Second World War, it is used chiefly by pleasure craft.

HARBOURS ON BRAS D'OR LAKE

The road through St. Peters crosses the canal linking the harbour with St. Peters Inlet on Bras d'Or Lake. The lake is also linked to the sea at the north by channels either side of Boularderie Island. It has been home to the Mi'kmaq for thousands of years, offering security and sustenance to them as they hunted in the forests and fished and gathered molluscs on its shores. Indigenous placenames can be found around the lake, and four Mi'kmaw communities are now established at traditional sites. More recent settlement around the lake dates from the nineteenth century when British immigrants, chiefly from Scotland, began to form communities on its shores and particularly around its many little coves and harbours.

Eskasoni

The Mi'kmaq named an area on the lake We'kwistoqnik, meaning "where the fir trees are plentiful." In early days, their encampments were widely scattered around the Bras d'Or Lake, and Eskasoni harbour was just one of many places where they built their wigwams. When British settlers encroached on Mi'kmaw territory on the lake to establish farms and villages, tracts of land were set aside as reserves. The Eskasoni Reserve was created in 1834, centred on the sheltered harbour behind Goat Island. In 1871 there were a hundred and twenty-five people living there, but by the end of the century the number had declined to about eighty. The Mi'kmaq lived by their traditional methods, depending on the lake and the forest for all their daily needs. The influence of white settlements and colonial government began to increase and encroach on their social and cultural framework. In the 1940s, when government policies resulted in the relocation of many more Mi'kmaq to Eskasoni, government aid failed to provide adequate housing and employment, leaving families without means of earning a living. There were dramatic and disastrous outcomes: their children were forced to attend residential schools, thereby ripping apart families, and separating the younger generation from their language and culture.

The tide began to turn with the establishment in 1958 of a Band Council that took control of the community's affairs. Under its leadership, the Eskasoni First Nation developed its resources, bringing some prosperity, although there is still a high level of unemployment. Today, the Eskasoni First Nation, near the head of West Eskasoni Harbour, is the largest Indigenous community in the Atlantic provinces. A community-owned seafood processing plant with its main office and wharf overlook the harbour. A tourist initiative is developing, and a bridge on the harbour leads to the Goat Island Trail, where Mi'kmaw interpreters share their people's

The provincially operated Ross Ferry leaving Big Harbour in 1948.

history and culture with visitors. Modern fishing boats have replaced birchbark canoes, and the harbour is a focal point of the economy.

Big Harbour

While the Eskasoni harbour is increasingly busy, to the northwest lies the now sleepy cove named Big Harbour. To find it, we leave Highway 105 at Big Hill and take a long country road to where the derelict remains of a ferry wharf are the only reminder of Big Harbour's busier days.

The Big Harbour road and the wharf were once an important part of the provincial highway system. For almost a century, a ferry between Big Harbour and Ross Ferry on Boularderie Island carried traffic from western Cape Breton towards Sydney and the industrial heartland of Cape Breton.

As in other areas of Nova Scotia, the Big Harbour ferry was originally operated by private individuals who received subsidies from the government, and in early days when traffic was light, they ran the ferry as a sideline from their regular occupations. The first ferries were probably small boats also used for fishing. There were no regular schedules, and the boats only crossed as travellers came along. The last of the private ferrymen was Jess Matheson, who operated his boat until about 1925.

At this time, the provincial government assumed responsibility for the ferry, maintaining the wharves and running a regular motorized service that provided employment for the community. In winter, the operators often had to clear and maintain a channel through the ice. By the late 1950s, with better roads and developing tourist traffic, the ferry could not keep up with demand. The Seal Island Bridge was completed in 1961, and the ferry was discontinued. It had provided work for people in Big Harbour, and with its closure many moved away, leaving their homes to summer residents.

Baddeck

One of the most-visited and well-known towns on Bras d'Or Lake is Baddeck. The Alexander Graham Bell Museum tells the story of its most famous resident. It is also the administrative centre for Victoria County, whose officials meet in its historic courthouse. There is plenty of accommodation for travellers, and a boatyard and marina on its little harbour.

The name Baddeck is thought to come from the Mi'kmaw name A'pitekwik or Epitekwik, meaning "a place with an island nearby." French missionaries came from Sainte-Anne in the 1630s to work among the Indigenous inhabitants living on the shores of the bay. The Mi'kmaq in this area reside mostly in the nearby Wagmatcook First Nation Reserve where they have a cultural centre and several community-operated businesses.

The first British grantees in Baddeck came in the late eighteenth and early nineteenth centuries. Captain Jonathan Jones, a Loyalist, received land on the Baddeck River, and Scottish settlers soon began developing farms in the surrounding countryside. James Duffus first settled on the nearby island and opened a store. Later he obtained an additional grant on the mainland, where the present town now stands.

In 1833, William Kidston came to Baddeck after being shipwrecked on his way from Halifax to Scotland, and remained there. After Duffus's death, he managed his business and later married his widow. The island became known as Kidston Island. Charles Campbell, manager of the island store, established a store of his own on the mainland in 1841, where he also set up a shipyard and ran a shipping business.

When Victoria County was created in 1851, Baddeck became the shire town and served as a trading port for the surrounding farming area. The settlement quickly expanded, and businesses grew up. Ships came to the wharf bringing passengers and goods, and left with produce, cattle, and sheep from the nearby farms. By the end of the nineteenth century, Baddeck was prospering.

Alexander Graham Bell, the inventor of the telephone, arrived in Baddeck with his family in 1885. They built their summer home on their estate of Beinn Bhreagh across the bay from the town, where Bell began to experiment with tetrahedral kites, hydrofoils, and eventually with airplanes, with his colleague, Casey Baldwin, and a team of workers. Baddeck Bay was the scene of many of his early experiments with kites, and of two major achievements. In 1909, his airplane, the Silver Dart, piloted by John Alexander Douglas McCurdy, was launched from the ice on the bay. This event brought Baddeck to the public's attention as it was the first powered flight in Canada. One of the hydrofoils that Bell developed in the bay established a world speed record for watercraft in 1919. Bell died at his home in Baddeck in 1922. His achievements are commemorated at the Alexander Graham Bell National Historic Site.

Today, the Trans-Canada Highway serves Baddeck, and vessels rarely come to its wharf with goods and passengers. Tourist accommodation, services, and entertainment attract summer visitors to the town and bring employment to the community's residents. Baddeck remains the economic and cultural centre of the region. There are businesses that repair and refit boats of all kinds, and a yacht club, since the lake is a sailing paradise, in summer and fall. In 2019, Baddeck hosted a small Norwegian cruise ship, perhaps inaugurating a new tourism initiative for the harbour.

ST. ANNS HARBOUR

Tourists headed for the Cabot Trail from Sydney usually take the ferry from the foot of Kellys Mountain, where a long gravel beach at the southern end of St. Anns Bay creates a sheltered harbour that the Mi'kmaq named M'tleegalitek. This is another very significant area for the Mi'kmaq. In Indigenous lore, Kluskap, the Mi'kmaw archetype, is said to have lived in a cave at Cape Dauphin, near the harbour entrance. As a result, the traditions that have been passed down through generations of Mi'kmaq affirm that since Kluskap left this world here, this is the centre of the universe, and many people come here for spiritual renewal and sacred ceremonies.

The French came to the harbour in 1629. After capturing a Scottish military outpost at Baleine, Captain Charles Daniel brought the soldiers as prisoners to the head of St. Anns Bay where he established a settlement that he named Havre Sainte-Anne. He had the Scots build a fort with living quarters, a chapel, and a powder magazine. He then took them to England, leaving forty of his men to garrison the fort, with two Jesuit missionaries. He returned with more Jesuits and additional settlers and ran a trading post for some years. The Jesuits operated their first North American mission at Havre Sainte-Anne until 1641, when the garrison was transferred to the French outpost at Placentia, Newfoundland. The remaining civilians continued to make their living by fishing and trading with the Mi'kmaq.

In the early 1650s Simon Denys de la Trinité, in partnership with his brother Nicolas, set up a fishing station in the harbour. It was short-lived: like his brother, Simon was caught up in the disputes among rival French merchants, captured, and taken to Quebec, where he remained.

Havre Sainte-Anne stayed in obscurity until 1713, when France finally lost mainland Acadie and set about fortifying its remaining colony of Île Royale. Sainte-Anne, now renamed Port Dauphin, was considered as a site for the main fortress before Louisbourg was chosen. A subsidiary defence, Fort Dauphin was built on the south side of the harbour entrance. It was manned by troops transferred from the garrison at Placentia, which had been taken over by the British. A military barracks, a powder magazine, a forge, and a lime kiln were built. The governor of Île Royale, Pasteur de Costebelle, established a residence, and civilian dwellings spread along the shore. Fishing crews dried their catch on the beach that protects the harbour.

Port Dauphin was a busy place by the 1730s, as gypsum and limestone were mined at the head of the harbour, and shipbuilding and repairs were carried out on the north shore. All this came to an end with the fall of Louisbourg, when the residents were removed, and Port Dauphin was destroyed by English naval vessels.

In 1819, a ship came into the harbour to shelter from a severe storm. Its passengers included a fiery Scottish preacher named Norman McLeod and a group of his followers, who had left Pictou in search of a new home far from what he considered the worldly wickedness of the townspeople. Having surveyed the scene, McLeod decided to remain and was joined by more of his flock the following year. The Gaelic-speaking settlers built homes for themselves, and a house and a church for McLeod, at the head of what was now known as St. Anns Harbour. Most people made their livings from farming and fishing, while John Munro established a shipyard and lumber business on the north shore. The community was encouraged to be self-sufficient, and to avoid contact with the outside world. McLeod terrorized his congregations with threats of hellfire, but they flocked to hear his preaching.

Over the next thirty years, McLeod became increasingly tyrannical and dissatisfaction grew among the residents. Matters came to a head in 1848 when the potato crop failed, and food supplies ran low. Munro's store would have been their lifeline to help from elsewhere, but the minister had denounced him for allegedly carrying rum in one of his vessels and had ordered a boycott of his business.

The solution to McLeod's problems came with a letter from one of his sons in Australia, persuading him to abandon St. Anns and move with his followers halfway around the world. In 1851, McLeod's ship *Margaret* sailed out of the harbour with 140 passengers. Many more followed later. Of those who had decided to stay, many drifted away, leaving behind a small fishing community.

Meanwhile, the settlement of Englishtown had grown up at the harbour entrance, where once Fort Dauphin had stood. It was also settled by Scots, but these were English-speaking Lowlanders, hence the name. They too made their living by fishing and by subsistence farming. They were joined by some Highlanders, among them one Norman MacAskill, who came to Englishtown in about 1830 with his family. His son Angus would later become famous as "Giant" MacAskill, whose feats of strength became legendary. He appeared in shows in North America, the West Indies, Britain, and Europe before returning home to operate a gristmill in Englishtown, where his life is commemorated in the Giant MacAskill Museum.

During the twentieth century the fishery that had sustained the Englishtown community declined drastically and many families moved away, but a new transportation initiative made the harbour a destination for travellers from all over the world. In 1929, a ferry was established to carry cars across the narrow entrance to the harbour. Once used to dry fish, St. Anns Beach is now part of the shortcut on the way to the scenic Cabot Trail. In 1936 the Gaelic College was established at the head of the harbour to preserve the area's Gaelic culture and traditions. It has grown from modest beginnings to an institution that attracts thousands of students annually. St. Anns Harbour is a popular place, and the Englishtown ferry is said to be the busiest in the province.

CHÉTICAMP

The Cabot Trail leads over the Cape Breton Highlands to the west coast of the island, to the largest Acadian community in Cape Breton, where French is still the first language of most residents. Before the community of Chéticamp was established, the area was named Awja'tu'j by the Mi'kmaq.

The village is tucked in behind Chéticamp Island, which is joined to the mainland by a narrow neck of land. This creates a sheltered harbour, although for many years a sandbar blocked its northern entrance to all but small boats. In early days, visiting fishing vessels would have moored in the cove behind the southern tip of the island—La Pointe—where the beach was suitable for drying cod.

Nicolas Denys visited the place that he called Le Chadye, probably in the 1650s, at a time when he had extensive fishing rights on Cape Breton Island. He described the long cove with its beach of sand mixed with pebbles, with a saltwater pond behind, and rocks on both sides. He observed that the sea was very rich with cod, which attracted fishing vessels, but they were often lost due to lack of shelter.

One hundred years later Samuel Holland's report mentions staging and huts on the shore, and shelter for small boats. He wrote, "Chetican or Macclesfield Harbour…provided shelter for small fishing craft, many of which the French built here." English names replaced many French ones on Holland's maps, and this name was probably intended to honour the Earl of Macclesfield. Nevertheless, the French name prevailed, and Macclesfield was erased.

A permanent Acadian settlement began to develop at Chéticamp in the 1780s. The settlers came by circuitous routes. Some had lived on Île Saint-Jean (Prince Edward Island) until it came under British rule, some returned from exile in France, while others came from the mainland or from elsewhere in Cape Breton. Most families operated small subsistence farms, but they made their living from the sea.

It was not an easy living. Some of the newcomers were Jerseymen—agents of the Robin Company from the Channel Islands—who controlled much of the fishery in the Bay of Chaleur and Cape Breton and established a fishing station in Chéticamp in 1780. The company outfitted the fishing schooners and brought in many of the residents' necessities.

The Robin establishment was set up first at La Pointe, where the schooners anchored at a large wharf and brought their catches ashore. There were stages and sheds where employees worked long hours cutting and salting the fish. The women tended the flakes on which the cod was dried ready for marketing. They were paid with credit at the company store rather than in cash, so they were obliged to make their purchases there. Naturally, the wages were poor, prices were high, and people were frequently indebted to the company. Not only was fishing a dangerous occupation, but life on shore was full of challenges. These harsh conditions remained unchanged until after the First World War.

One former Robin employee, Jean Lelièvre, acquired land at Pointe-à-Cochon at the head of the harbour and formed his own company, opening a store in 1812 which operated on similar principles. In the mid-nineteenth century, Sam Lawrence, who owned a fishing company at Margaree, started his operation on the harbour, but times were changing. The Lawrence Company was bought by Charles Aucoin, who sold it in 1911 to the Matthews & Scott Company, which had a more humane attitude to its employees and paid them in cash.

In the late 1800s, an enterprising Pictou merchant opened a lobster cannery on the harbour, which was bought by the Lawrence Company, but closed a few years later. Other attempts to establish canneries lasted for only a short time, but the cod fishery remained active, and at the end of the nineteenth century there were twenty large schooners operating from the harbour.

In 1890 two lighthouses were installed to guide vessels, one at Pointe Enragé at the northern tip of the island, the other on the mainland. The island lighthouse is still standing but is no longer operating.

Ships were built on the harbour at Pointe-à-Cochon, but some people built boats on land and dragged them to the water. The story is told of Michel Maillet of nearby Petit Étang who built a big schooner on his land more than a kilometre from the sea and with the help of his neighbours and seventy-five pairs of oxen hauled it to the shore, where it was launched amid a crowd of spectators. It presumably went on to join the fleet of vessels operating from the harbour.

For many years, the sandbar across the harbour mouth had prevented all but the smallest vessels from entering, and ships had to transfer their cargo to dories to bring it ashore. At the instigation of the parish priest in 1874, the entrance was dredged with the help of the federal government and has since been maintained.

The first steamship to operate out of Chéticamp was a paddle steamer, which began a coastal service to Pictou in 1886, calling at ports in between. The service was quickly expanded to include the Magdalen Islands, and by 1909 there were routes to Halifax and Sydney.

The harbour remained busy with fishing and trading schooners, but changes came about in the twentieth century with the introduction of trawlers and boats with gas engines. The Robin business was transferred from La Pointe to the harbour in 1903. Refrigeration was introduced, at first simply for storing bait, but later as an alternative method of preserving fish.

The biggest change for the people of Chéticamp came about in 1915, when a group of fishers, tired of being exploited by the old companies, formed a co-operative. Based at the government wharf at La Pointe, they began in a

Fishermen unloading herring at Chéticamp, ca. 1955.

small way, canning lobster by hand at what was known as *"la petite Factorie de La Pointe."* With sales in Halifax, Charlottetown and Port Elgin, they were able to expand their business and their membership.

The Depression was hard on Chéticamp as many people who had found work in New England were laid off and returned home. In 1933, in order to revive the economy, the fishermen formed another co-operative, built a cannery and a wharf, and later, a store. The two co-operatives merged in 1940, and the harbour became the business centre of the community.

There was one industry that kept providing jobs—gypsum mining. Gypsum had been discovered nearby at the turn of the century, and in 1908, the Great Northern Mining Company's 5,000-ton freighter left the harbour with its mineral cargo. A few years later, the company went bankrupt and production ceased, but from 1923, the mine was worked sporadically by different companies, which gave a boost to the local economy. Between 1936 and the outbreak of the Second World War, the industry was successful, and quantities of gypsum were exported on large carriers.

In 1949, the provincial government built a public refrigeration plant for the fishery, which the co-operative bought out five years later with federal assistance. Modern warehouses were built on the co-operative store's wharf which, unfortunately, were destroyed by a fire in 1955. With a government loan, they were rebuilt at the harbour entrance, along with a second refrigeration plant. Two years later, a fish meal plant was added, making use of discarded fish parts.

When a moratorium was placed on the cod fishery in 1992, hard times returned to the harbour. The seal hunt that had provided an income for some residents became the subject of attacks and boycotts, and the economy slumped. It has revived with diversification of the catch and the development of the hospitality industry. The village lies on the popular Cabot Trail, and travellers are encouraged to stay and enjoy refreshment, and to visit the community's historic church and Les Trois Pignons, a museum of hooked rugs.

Fishing remains the chief occupation, though the focus has shifted from cod to snow crab and lobster. Boats still tie up at the wharf at La Pointe, where a breakwater provides protection. The busy port of La Digue, at the harbour entrance, is the centre of the fishery, with wharves, boat storage sheds, a launching ramp, and the office of the Harbour Authority of Chéticamp. Another little fishing wharf lies within the harbour. A boatyard builds fishing boats and carries out repairs just across the water from Pointe-à-Cochon, the original shipbuilding site. The village is the centre of Acadian culture in northern Cape Breton.

Eastern Shore

Back on the mainland, Nova Scotia's beautiful Eastern Shore is probably the least- visited region in the province, and is quite sparsely populated. For those who find their way there, its spectacular scenery and its history make the journey worthwhile. The tourist route called Marine Drive, between Guysborough and Halifax, runs by the heads of the many inlets where Mi'kmaq and Europeans first met and traded. These harbours have sheltered Basque and French fishermen since the 1550s, and some of the first land-based fisheries were established there. Records of early attempts at agriculture and permanent settlements can be traced back to the seventeenth century. The area also saw disputes among rival French entrepreneurs over fishing and fur-trading rights, clashes between Mi'kmaq and Europeans who were usurping their territory, and skirmishes between the French and New Englanders over access to the valuable fishery.

After British rule was definitively established in Nova Scotia, fishing and shipbuilding communities developed along the shore from Cole Harbour to Canso and Guysborough.The nineteenth and early twentieth centuries were their most prosperous times, but like their counterparts in other areas of Nova Scotia, these towns and villages suffered from the decline of shipbuilding and competition from larger urban sawmills. With the collapse of the cod fishery, which had been a major source of employment, workers left to seek a living elsewhere. Today, populations have declined, but fishing boats bring in a more diversified catch to the harbours, and the hospitality industry stimulates the economy as the Eastern Shore's unspoiled scenery and interesting local museums attract tourists.

CHEDABUCTO BAY

The name Chedabucto comes from the Mi'kmaw word Sedabooktook, meaning "running far back." The bay extends from Cape Canso to Guysborough, at the mouth of the Milford Haven River. Both Canso and Guysborough were early French fishing bases. Fishing remained the mainstay of the economy for many years, and Canso's fishing boats are still a valued source of income.

Canso

Remote Cape Canso is the easternmost point of mainland Nova Scotia. The Mi'kmaw name for the area is Kamsok, which the French adapted to Campseau or Canceau. Canso Harbour lies between Durells Island and the mainland and is an active fishing port today, but often in times past fishing boats anchored for the season in small coves among the Canso Islands.

In the seventeenth century Canso was often the first stopping point for ships from Europe bound for Acadie or the St. Lawrence River. It was also a point of departure, and it was here that Champlain and the disappointed Port Royal colonists assembled in 1607 to board the ship that would take them back to France.

In 1632, Nicolas Le Creux du Breuil was sent to Canceau from LaHève to establish Fort Saint-François, with a small garrison to protect French interests—sometimes against their own countrymen. Fur-trading rights were officially limited to those authorized by the Company of New France, but this restriction was frequently ignored. Canceau was the scene of an incident in 1635, when a fishing captain, Jean Thomas, incited some Mi'kmaq with whom he was illegally trading to attack the fort. A skirmish followed, during which Le Creux was wounded. Thomas was captured and sent first to LaHève, and then to France for trial.

In 1690, New England fishing crews were granted licences to fish in Acadian waters, and during the eighteenth century the Canso fishery became increasingly popular among New Englanders. French and English boats often fished peaceably side by side, but as the century progressed, the harbour was the scene of several confrontations. In 1718 Cyprian Southack and Thomas Smart in the ship *Squirrel* raided the islands and seized French ships and their cargo. In 1720, the tables were turned when French and Mi'kmaw boats raided the New Englanders' fishing stations.

There were more raids over the following years. The British built a fort on Grassy Island to protect their interests, and a small settlement grew up there, with fishing and trading vessels using its little harbour. In 1720, residents were alarmed when Bartholomew Roberts, a notorious Welsh pirate known as Black Bart, visited Canso in his sloop *Fortune* with its black flag flying. He was on his way to carry out operations in Newfoundland when he seized the opportunity to raid Canso on his way past. Fortunately, he did not stay long.

France and Britain were at war again in 1744 when Canso was attacked by soldiers from Louisbourg, aided by a Mi'kmaw band. The British commandant was taken by surprise and forced to surrender. The men of the garrison were taken prisoner, and the fort and settlement were burnt down. The following year, British troops mustered at Canso before besieging Louisbourg.

When preparations were being made to bring New England settlers to Nova Scotia in the 1760s, Charles Morris laid out a town plot on the mainland beside the harbour. It was to be called Wilmot, in honour of the lieutenant-governor, but old habits die hard, and the town would be soon be known by the familiar name of Canso. Its residents quickly took up fishing and trading.

During the American Revolution, Canso was frequently under attack. American privateers repeatedly raided the harbour, and there were also raids by more regular forces, such as George Washington's Marblehead Regiment, which attacked the harbour in 1775. The following year saw two raids led by John Paul Jones. He sailed into the harbour in September and destroyed, burned, or captured several vessels, as well as damaging property on shore. Two months later, he raided the community again, seizing a small schooner, and burning a transport vessel and a warehouse where whale oil was stored. Another privateer destroyed the harbour's fishery facilities in 1779. Canso's economy was in a shambles but the residents rebuilt their lives, and once the war was over they set about re-establishing their fishing industry. By the beginning of the nineteenth century the town had recovered, and the fishing crews and families prospered for many years.

Canso also became the western end of the telegraph cables under the Atlantic between Ireland and North America. The first cable came ashore in the harbour and a station in Canso town was opened by Western Union in 1881, while a second station was operated by Commercial Cable just outside the town, at Hazel Hill, from 1884.

The collapse of the cod fishery and the port's geographical isolation brought hard times to Canso in the late twentieth century. As changing technology made their equipment obsolete, both cable companies closed their operations, one in 1955, the other in 1962, and their employees left.

Today, the reduced population makes a living from a recovering and more diversified fishery. Fishing boats again line the wharf at Canso Harbour, especially during the lobster season. A shrimp fishery has also been established. An exciting event from time to time on Canso's Fisherman's Wharf is the landing of a large tuna, a big attraction for tourists. Visitors come each summer to attend the Stan Rogers Folk Festival, and to visit the Canso Islands National Historic Site which recalls the harbour's long fishing history.

Guysborough

Due west of Canso, at the head of Chedabucto Bay, is Guysborough Harbour. Protected by a long sandbar, it lies at the estuary of the Milford Haven River. This was the site of one of the earliest fishing communities, although some people claim its history goes back much farther. It is said that Prince Henry Sinclair, Earl of the Orkneys, came to these shores in 1398, but like many legends, it lacks authenticity. What is more certain is that the area had been well known to European sailors for many years before Nicolas Denys acquired rights from the Company of New France to set up a land-based cod fishery and trading post that he called Chedabouctou, the French version of its Mi'kmaw name.

When Denys came to establish his headquarters and processing station on the west side of the harbour, in the late 1650s, the area was part of the French colony of Acadie. There were stages where the fish was brought in, benches where it was gutted, tubs for salting, and containers where the livers were pressed to extract oil. Nearby were the flakes on which the fish was dried. During the fishing season, the harbour was a hive of activity. All summer long, boats sailed out to the fishing grounds and returned to unload their catches.

Some of Denys's men lived year-round at Chedabouctou, cutting wood and clearing land on the west side of the harbour for farming to support the community, and maintaining the buildings and equipment. Even when their farms became productive, they needed goods from France, so Denys's ship returned each spring with fresh supplies.

Unfortunately, another French merchant had been granted fishing and trading rights around St. Marys River, in the area which abutted onto Denys's concession. The boundary between the two seems to have been ill-defined, and in 1667 Sieur de la Giraudière laid claim to Chedabouctou and seized Denys's supply ship, leaving him without provisions. Denys fortified the settlement and tried to defend it, but his buildings were destroyed, and he was forced to surrender. He travelled back to France and appealed to the Company of New France. Although they upheld his claim, the damage incurred meant that he was never able to rebuild his fishery at Chedabouctou.

In the 1680s another French entrepreneur, Clerbaud Bergier, re-established the Chedabouctou fishing station, and worked the abandoned farmland. Bergier, too, was caught up in commercial rivalries, as New Englanders also obtained fishing rights in the area and resented the French presence. To defend his settlement, he replaced Denys's old fortifications with Fort Saint-Louis, on a point

Fishing boats at a Guysborough wharf, ca. 1900.

overlooking the harbour. Despite this, New Englanders successfully raided and pillaged Chedabouctou in 1688. Two years later, Cyprian Southack led another New England attack. A French officer with twelve soldiers fought off the attackers for several hours before firebombs destroyed the fort.

About three hundred Acadians were living and fishing in the area and had rebuilt the fort by 1718 when Southack again sailed into the bay on HMS *Squirrel* and besieged the settlement, killing some of its defenders. The raiders were beaten back until British troops landed farther down the bay and attacked by land. Southack looted and burned the village and took Acadian prisoners to the Canso Islands, where they were released without food or extra clothing. Some residents were able to escape to Île Madame, and any remaining at the time of the Expulsion were deported.

For some years afterwards, little was heard of the harbour at the head of the bay. Fourteen Acadian families returned to farm and fish in the area in 1764, and a small English-speaking community also grew up. After the American Revolution, Loyalist settlers, including disbanded soldiers and Free Blacks, came to the harbour. Some of them came from the failed settlement at Port Mouton, which had originally been called Guysborough in honour of Governor General Sir Guy Carleton, and they brought the name with them.

Among the Loyalists was William Campbell, about whom John Grant tells a romantic story in his book, *Historic Guysborough*. It seems that, as Campbell was about to disembark in 1784, he noticed a girl working among the fish flakes on the shore and announced that she was to be his future wife. Sure enough, they were married the following year. Campbell received a water lot, but his wife no longer worked on the fish flakes as he turned his attention to law, became an attorney, and held several public offices before moving to Cape Breton.

The Guysborough settlers made a living with subsistence farms, as well as from lumbering and fishing. Throughout the nineteenth century, the harbour was busy with boats bringing in their catches for processing in local plants. Shipyards built vessels for fishing and trade. Guysborough merchants exported lumber, fish, and fish oil. Livestock was shipped to Newfoundland. Wharves and warehouses lined the waterfront; there was a customs house, and operations were supervised by various officials, including a collector of customs, a receiver of wrecks, and an inspector of fish oil. From 1830 until 1955, packet boats sailed regularly from Guysborough Harbour to Arichat. A similar service to Halifax operated between the 1840s and 1880.

In 1873, the area experienced what was known as the August Gale—probably a hurricane—which destroyed wharves and property. Rebuilding took place, but towards the end of the nineteenth century the fishery was already declining. Shipbuilding slowed, trading dwindled, and many people left in search of work elsewhere.

During the First World War, the harbour became more active with a revival in the fishery, and pit props (beams used to prop up the roofs of tunnels in coal mines) were sent to England when European sources were cut off. But during the Depression, although some fish and pulpwood were still exported, the population continued to decline.

Today, the once-busy waterfront has become a marina, and many tourists visit the area to fish for salmon and trout in the local rivers. Many of Guysborough's colourful historic buildings are still standing. Among them is the Jost's Wharf building, a reminder of the days when this was a busy trading port.

TOR BAY

Why do we find the name Savalette (or Savalet) recurring in communities around Tor Bay? Off the beaten track for many Nova Scotians, this beautiful area south of

Chedabucto Bay was among the first frequented by Europeans. One of the earliest testimonies to their activities is Marc Lescarbot's account of his meeting with a Basque fishing captain in 1607. Lescarbot and his companions were on their way to Canso when, he wrote:

> We arrived within four leagues of Campseau, at a port, where a good old man of Saint John de Luz, called Captain Savalet, received us with all the kindness in the world. And forasmuch as this port (which is little, but very fair) hath no name, I have qualified it in my Geographical Map with the name of Savalet. This good honest man told us that the same voyage was the forty-second voyage that he had made into these parts.

Savalette had a crew of sixteen people working for him, fishing in small boats and bringing their catch to dry on shore. He sailed home every fall in his eighty-ton vessel, which he said could carry "100,000 dry fishes." Savalette's many seasons of fishing push the date of his first voyage across the Atlantic back to the 1560s.

Champlain also mentions meeting Savalette when he was engaged in fishing among the islands. Both men refer to the French naming his fishing base Port Savalette, which has been identified as Whitehead, but is often applied to the whole of Tor Bay. Captain Savalette has been designated by the Canadian Government as a Person of National Historic Significance, and his name is still remembered in the area.

Savalette was among the first Europeans to fish regularly along Nova Scotia's Eastern Shore. Vessels not only from the Basque country but also from France and other countries frequented the waters of Tor Bay every summer. Early fishers either salted down their catches in their ships' holds, or dried the salted fish on the beaches before packing it in barrels to carry back to their home ports in the fall. Permanent fishing settlements were not yet established.

In 1797, a group of Acadians who had initially settled at Chezzetcook after the Expulsion received grants on Tor Bay. They included the Bellefontaine, Richard, Pellerin, Manette, Lavendier, Petitpas, Boudreau, David, Roi, and Bonnevie families. They settled around the little harbours of Larrys River, Charlos Cove, and Port Felix, where other families soon joined them. According to Brad Pellerin, Larrys River was named after an Irishman who was living in a log cabin on the east bank of the river, and Charlos Cove after Charles Richard, one of the original settlers. Port Felix, originally called Havre Mélasse because a keg of molasses had washed up there, was re-named to honour Father Felix van Blerk, the parish priest in the 1860s.

By the 1930s, there were over two thousand Acadians living around Tor Bay. Some people chose to leave when the fishery declined, but fishing boats can still be seen around the bay, profiting from the busy lobster season and a more diversified catch.

The area is isolated from other Acadian communities, and today, only a few of the older residents speak French. They are proud of their history: Place Savalette in Port Felix is a National Historic Park commemorating the meeting between the Basque captain and Champlain, and every year at Larry's River the Festival Savalette celebrates Tor Bay's Acadian heritage. There, too, a series of painted rocks represent historical scenes from Champlain's time onwards. The festival and the beautiful unspoiled scenery around the bay attract visitors to the area, and tourism is a growing industry for the Acadian harbours of Tor Bay.

COUNTRY HARBOUR AND ISAACS HARBOUR

After leaving Tor Bay, the main highway along the Eastern Shore to Halifax touches many long inlets that have sheltered vessels for hundreds of years. The road skirts Isaacs Harbour shortly before reaching Country Harbour. The two harbours come together in a wide exit to the sea. All that most people see of Country Harbour is the scenic view from the provincially operated ferry that crosses one of the longest estuaries on the Eastern Shore, avoiding a long detour around it.

There were once Indigenous settlements on both harbours, and the Mi'kmaq called the area Moukodome. It continued to be called Mocodome for many years after European vessels came there. By the mid-eighteenth century, Country Harbour was known by its present name, while Isaacs Harbour took its name from a Black Loyalist settler, Isaac Webb, who lived on the east side on what is still called Webbs Cove.

After the American Revolution, a contingent of disbanded soldiers came to Country Harbour, intending to establish farms. They had loaded two vessels with food supplies and building materials. The *Nymph* sailed into the harbour on Christmas Day, 1753, and her passengers came ashore. Their second ship, the *Argo*, was blown off course and limped in later, having lost her deck-load of lumber in the storm. From this inauspicious beginning, the newcomers attempted to create a settlement in the depths of winter. They hastily built log cabins but the homes were leaky and damp, and many people died. Without the help of the Mi'kmaq, even fewer would have survived. They named their settlement Mount Misery.

As the name suggests, conditions were harsh. Many of the survivors lacked farming experience, and deterred by the hardships, left after a short time. When spring came, fewer than thirty-five families remained. Those who stayed became lumbermen, farmers, and fishermen, in scattered properties around the harbour and farther up the river.

Captain John Leggatt bought up some of the land that had been abandoned and established a small settlement on the eastern shore behind Mount Misery. He operated a store and built a large house where he raised his family. Other settlers built homes there, operated stores and warehouses, and established other businesses including a tannery, a carding mill, and a sawmill. Lumber export became the major industry of the community that was known as Stormont. Country Harbour's residents suffered a setback in 1811 when a hurricane destroyed homes, along with ships at the wharves. The settlement was in ruins and people began to leave. The few who remained struggled to rebuild their homes and their lives. Isaac Webb and his family were abandoned when their employer left. They subsequently moved to the neighbouring harbour, which took Isaac's name.

Other families began to come to Isaacs Harbour in the early 1830s, and the community of Isaacs Harbour grew quickly. From 1840 to 1880 there was a flourishing shipbuilding industry in both harbours. By 1870, over thirty ships—mostly schooners and a few clipper ships—had been built. The community was more prosperous and more cohesive than the scattered households around the larger Country Harbour, and some residents of Stormont moved there.

There was excitement in May 1844 when the ship *Saladin*, carrying guano and a large amount of gold, silver, and copper from Valparaiso, was found stranded on Harbour Island at the entrance to the harbour. It turned out that six members of the crew had mutinied, taken over the ship, and murdered the captain and the other officers, crew, and passengers. The mutineers were taken to Halifax, where they were charged with piracy. Three of them were found guilty of murder and hanged, while the others pleaded that they had been coerced into taking part and escaped with their lives.

The discovery of gold on the east side of Isaacs Harbour in the 1860s brought an influx of hopeful prospectors to the area and a major shift in its economy. The initial gold rush in both harbours lasted for only a few years, but merchants established stores and wharves, supplies were brought in for the workers, and ships unloaded coal to fuel the mining operations. By the mid-1870s the main rush was over, leaving abandoned mines around the area. One mine remained operational at Goldboro, where merchants operated a cluster of stores and wharves. Mining continued in the Goldboro area until the 1940s, and gold exploration continues today.

For many years the most practical way to travel in this area was by water, and even today, the ferry service that crosses Country Harbour is an important part of the highway system. But roads have superseded coastal vessels and deep-sea fishing vessels now bring their catches into the harbour for transfer to refrigerated trucks. The working population of both harbours has dwindled; some people commute to work in other communities, and their boats are mostly pleasure craft. Passengers on the ferry have unspoiled views of this magnificent harbour, and in summer, vacationers come to enjoy its beauty and peace.

ST. MARYS RIVER

Visitors to the historic Sherbrooke Village on St. Marys River stroll among a collection of heritage buildings operated by the Nova Scotia Museum, where costumed interpreters recreate the life of the nineteenth-century community that grew up around the lumber export industry. But this is just part of the harbour's history.

In 1655, a French entrepreneur, Charles de la Giraudière, came to the area that the Mi'kmaq named Naboosakun. He built a small fortified settlement at the head of the long estuary of the river he named Sainte-Marie, where he exported fish and furs. The community that grew up at Port Sainte-Marie made a living from hunting, fishing, and fur trading. The settlement was raided by English vessels in 1669, the French were driven out, and the fort destroyed, but the river retained its name. Although the river was rich in salmon and there were valuable timber resources all around, it would be over one hundred years before development took place.

Remnants of the fort were still visible in the early 1800s when some Irish settlers came to the harbour. They farmed, fished, and established a sawmill on the east side of the harbour. They were joined in 1814 by David Archibald, who bought the mill, opened a store, and began a lumber export business. This was the beginning of the village of Sherbrooke. In the late 1820s, William Scarth Moorsom visited the village, which he described as a "modest assemblage of twenty cottages." He went on to describe the harbour:

> The river is ninety yards broad at this spot, with a depth of twelve feet at low water. Vessels of six hundred tons can anchor securely two miles lower down; and for six miles from its mouth the channel is never closed in winter. Small craft under one hundred tons are used for this navigation by the settlers, and during the year 1828 six vessels of this weight were built between Sherbrooke and the sea.…Two small fishing establishments have recently been formed by

private speculation in this port; the craft employed in them carry lumber or produce to Halifax in April, and there fit out for the Labrador coast; this speculation is proceeding prosperously.

Ships were built on the river throughout the nineteenth century, and vessels laden with lumber continued to sail down the estuary. Many were bound for Britain, and returned with cloth, glass, and hardware for the merchants of Sherbrooke, oakum for shipbuilding, and salt for the fishery. Fish was processed in the village and exported on vessels that brought back goods from the West Indies. Coastal trading ships sailed along the eastern seaboard and to ports on the St. Lawrence.

There was a flurry of excitement when gold was discovered on the west side of the harbour in the 1860s. Speculators rushed to Sherbrooke and the town of Goldenville sprang up almost overnight. A bridge was built across the head of the harbour to replace an earlier ferry, and loading wharves were built on the banks of the river. Like other gold-rush towns, Goldenville saw only a brief period of prosperity before its seams became less productive, and most of the prospectors moved away. Sherbrooke had benefitted from this surge in its economy, but quickly returned to its former occupations of sawmilling, lumber exporting, and fishing. Recently, there has been renewed interest in the area's potential gold resources.

There is still some lumbering and fishing in the area, but today, trucks have replaced ships, and big trading vessels no longer leave the harbour. Sherbrooke Village attracts tourists and provides summer employment for residents. The McDonald Bros. Sawmill and other historic buildings have been preserved, and the demonstrations of many traditional trades and crafts immerse visitors in the life of Sherbrooke at the height of its industrial prosperity.

LISCOMB HARBOUR

The road down the Eastern Shore winds along the north shore of Liscomb Harbour to Liscomb Mills at the mouth of Liscomb River. The harbour was called Medagavik by Mi'kmaq, and the British called it Franklin's Harbour, but eventually it took on its present name. Hemloe Island separates Little Liscomb Harbour from the main harbour, and Spanish Ship Bay is an inlet to the north. Liscomb Island lies at the harbour mouth. A series of small settlements surround the harbour, with Liscomb Mills and West Liscomb at its head.

Settlement on the harbour began in 1765 when land for a fishing lot was granted to George Smith and his brothers, who established a settlement on the south side, protected by Liscomb Island and close to rich fishing grounds. Land on the northeast side of the harbour was surveyed for Richard Spry, the commander-in-chief of the British Navy's North American Station. A few years later he was transferred to the Mediterranean and abandoned his property at Liscomb. Because he had not fulfilled the terms of his grant by developing it and establishing settlers, Spry's land around the harbour was escheated, and granted to Loyalists in 1784. Some of them found it too hard to make a living and left, but others farmed the land, and built wharves and fish stores on Little Liscomb Harbour. Judge William Spry received an early grant nearby, but he was appointed Governor of Barbados in 1767 and he, too, left Nova Scotia. His sister had an interest in the grant, but did not develop it, and that property, too, was escheated.

A more stable period began in the late 1790s, when James Umlach (Hemloe) and his father-in-law, James McDaniel, began to use Amelia Island, now Hemloe Island, as a fishing base. When William Spry's land became available in 1810, Hemloe applied for and received a grant of two hundred acres on the mainland as well as Amelia and Hog Islands. By now, he was living on St. Marys River, so he transferred his Liscomb property to his sons, Henry and William Hemloe. It is said that the first general store in the area was opened on Hemloe Island. James Hemloe's daughter, Elizabeth, and her mariner husband, Christopher Redman, acquired land on the nearby point, now known as Redman's Head.

In the early 1800s, the population increased as people from Lunenburg County and elsewhere settled around the harbour and on the islands and became farmers, fishermen, and merchant mariners. Among them was Jacob Crooks, who came from LaHave to Liscomb Island, formerly known as Crooks Island, where he built a schooner and raised a family.

Some settlers were less successful. In 1817 a ship carrying Lord Dalhousie, the lieutenant-governor, anchored in the harbour and received a visit from "a poor fisher," a well-educated Irishman who had served in the army. He came to ask for a grant of the land where he was living with his wife and eleven children. Dalhousie wrote:

> His appearance is quite original, long, lanky white hair hanging over a very old and wrinkled head, a hat in rags, & often sewed together with rope yarns, a shirt of flannel, red and yellow pieces patched—a pair of soldier's old pantaloons & no shoes....The Admiral gave him a Bag of Biscuit, the sailors loaded him with cloathes, & he went away as drunk as he well could be.

Boats in Liscomb Harbour in the twentieth century.

Not all the inhabitants were such colourful characters.

In 1837, the brigantine *Gratitude*, out of St. John's, Newfoundland, was wrecked on Liscomb Island. The harbour entrance was dangerous in bad weather, but there was no lighthouse on the island until 1872, when Jacob Crook's son Seth became the keeper. More recently, in 2012, an unknown vessel dropped a group of ten Lithuanians on the island's shore. They were found by the local residents, taken to Halifax, and eventually deported.

In the early nineteenth century, James Archibald built a mill at the head of the harbour, where a small settlement developed. Some residents worked in the mill and others cut lumber. Archibald's mill failed, but another entrepreneur, Alexander Sinclair, set up a mill and cut wood both for export and to support a shipyard on the harbour. The community became known as Liscomb Mills; there was plenty of work for lumbermen, mill workers, carpenters, and seamen, and for some years, the harbour was busy with ships carrying lumber away for export. But Sinclair's business failed in the late 1880s, and many people moved away. Today, Liscomb Mills is little more than a name on the map and a stopping place on the road.

Other settlements were established around the harbour. A busy fishing village grew up on Henry Hemloe's grant on Little Liscomb Harbour. The arm known as Spanish Ship Bay was first settled by Jacob McKinley in about 1813. The origin of the bay's name is obscure. Local lore suggests that a Spanish ship took refuge there

Visitors come to Tangier to enjoy the beauty of the harbour and its islands.

from pirates, ran aground on an island and was wrecked. Other accounts claim that the wrecked vessel was a Spanish pirate ship. McKinley's sons, John and Aaron, and others received grants on Spanish Ship Bay, where the residents became lumbermen, shipbuilders, fishers, and merchant seamen.

Today, except for a few fishing boats, all these activities around the harbour have come to an end. Vacationers visit Liscomb Mills for trout and salmon fishing in the river, while nature lovers enjoy hiking on the scenic Liscomb River Trail. The area's industrial past is largely forgotten.

TANGIER HARBOUR

Tangier Harbour was traditionally known to the Mi'kmaq as Wospegeak, meaning "the place of shining water." Its English name is said to commemorate the wreck of the schooner *Tangier*, in 1830. The first European settlers came in the late eighteenth century, and settled on the islands around the harbour, close to the Atlantic fishery, and on the mainland at the head of the harbour.

The scattered residents were living quietly, clearing land for farms, planting orchards, and fishing, until 1860, when Peter Mason discovered gold on the east side of the harbour, where the settlement of Tangier grew up. This was one of the earliest gold discoveries in Nova Scotia and resulted in the inevitable "gold rush" that brought prospectors and speculators to the harbour, along with hopeful people seeking employment as miners. The Strawberry Hill Mine that began production in the 1860s was the first underground mine in Nova Scotia. The gold was exported by ship from Tangier Harbour.

In 1861, Captain Campbell Hardy, an officer of the Royal Artillery stationed in Nova Scotia, described the mining settlement, known as Gold Street, as "an assemblage of wooden houses, or rather shanties, raised up at an expense of £2 or £3 in this country of cheap timber." That same year, Tangier received a visit from Queen Victoria's son, Prince Alfred, who toured the gold mine. An arch commemorating his visit overlooks the harbour in the little Graeme Ferguson Memorial Park.

Mining lasted, with diminishing returns, until 1919. Gold was originally exported by water, but later, rail transport took over. Operations were revived from time to time in the twentieth century, and mining companies have recently renewed interest in the area.

In 1956, a successful new fish-processing business started up in Tangier when a Danish couple, Jorgen Willy Krauch and his wife, began to operate the smokehouse that became known internationally for its smoked salmon and other seafood. The firm of J. Willy Krauch and Sons was maintained as a family business after Willy's death until 2015, when the Tangier operation was closed, and the brand was transferred to Comeau Seafoods in Saulnierville.

Some fishing is still carried on, though many of the farms and fishing wharves are now deserted. Tangier is better known today for the sea kayaking tours that bring visitors to its harbour.

COLE HARBOUR, LAWRENCETOWN, AND CHEZZETCOOK

Cole Harbour, the final stop on the way back to Halifax, is protected by its islands and its ever-changing sand dunes. It has been both shaped by humans and sculpted by the ocean. Unlike most of Nova Scotia's harbours, its economy has been based on the land more than on the sea, and its history is very different from that of other areas on the Eastern Shore. Today, most of its shores are part of Lawrencetown Coastal Heritage Provincial Park, including the Saltmarsh Trail and Rainbow Haven Beach on the sandbar that reaches across the harbour entrance. But long before the land around the harbour was set aside as a heritage and recreational area, it was the summer destination for the Mi'kmaq who called it Wonpaak—the place of still water. They camped here every summer, and harvested shellfish, berries, and game, until British settlement began to develop around the harbour.

Cole Harbour, Lawrencetown, and Chezzetcook form an interesting group of once-interconnected communities. Chezzetcook, the most easterly, lies on Chezzetcook Inlet, some distance from the other two. The original settlement of Lawrencetown was established east of Cole Harbour, while Upper Lawrencetown lies to the north, and the community of Cole Harbour on the western side.

Acadians were living in this area in the early 1750s, farming the land and harvesting hay from the extensive saltmarshes. When the authorities in Halifax were looking for a place to establish a Protestant farming community to feed the people of Halifax, they originally considered the Cole Harbour/Lawrencetown area as a possible site, but eventually established the Foreign Protestants in Lunenburg in 1753. One year later, however, Charles Morris surveyed the area "now to be called Lawrencetown," for British settlers. Twenty "gentlemen" were given grants to establish farms in the new settlement and provided with provisions for a year. The town of Lawrencetown was laid out east of Cole Harbour, on the western side of the narrow entrance to Lawrencetown Lake, and a road was constructed between Dartmouth and the town.

Meanwhile, the Acadians had moved on, to what Morris identified as Shillingcook, now Chezzetcook, from the Mi'kmaw name Sesetkook. By the time of the Expulsion, there were seven or eight families living around Chezzetcook Inlet's harbour, where they pursued their traditional farming methods on the marshland, fished, and traded with the Mi'kmaq.

Nobody, of course, had consulted the Mi'kmaq before laying out the settlement at Lawrencetown. Already smarting from Cornwallis's high-handed encroachment on their land in Halifax, they threatened this new establishment. A small fortification was built as protection from raids, but Lawrencetown was a long way from the garrison in Halifax, and the problem of providing security for the residents could not be overcome. By 1757 many people had abandoned the original Lawrencetown site and it would be some time before British settlers returned.

Chief Surveyor Charles Morris's notes on a map made in 1754 confusingly identify Cole Harbour as "Wompawk, by some called Muscodoboit, by others Cold Harbour." The name seems to have been determined by 1758, when James Cook, stationed in Halifax, drew "A Draught of the Harbour of Halifax and the Adjacent Coast", showing "Cole Harbour." It was depicted as shallow and sandy, "dry at low water," and with only a four-foot deep channel from its narrow entrance. This was clearly not suitable for large vessels, but smaller boats could make their way along channels cut by the little Salmon River and brooks flowing into the harbour.

Morris's map identifies areas that were "reserved for the fishery, ship-building and other publick uses" that were expected to be part of a developing economy. However, they lay outside the harbour, one on the ocean side of the sandspit that was at that time on the east side of the entrance to Cole Harbour, another at Fox (now Egg) Island, off the "Entrance into the Harbour of Lawrence Town, also a small Peninsula on the South West side of said Harbour." The fishing, shipbuilding, and merchant shipping industries did not develop at Cole Harbour as they did elsewhere in the province. Some small ships were built, and for a while lumber was exported, but most of the residents would turn to agriculture for a living.

Towards the turn of the century, a few people began to settle along the Lawrencetown Road, on the northern edge of Cole Harbour. During the 1800s the population spread to the original Lawrencetown area as threats of attack diminished. There was good farmland available there, and hay could be cut and livestock pastured on the salt marshes. Farms became productive and supplied the Halifax market with hay and vegetables, while lumber was cut and exported.

The Chezzetcook community was re-established in the 1760s when Acadians returned to Nova Scotia. However, when Loyalist refugees of English, Scottish, and German descent also received grants in the area, some Acadians left, fearing that the newcomers would encroach on their land. Others remained and continued to maintain their way of life. The Loyalist settlers took up farming and fishing, and like their Acadian neighbours, cut hay on the marshes for sale in Halifax. They established a sawmill at the head of the inlet that processed lumber for export. A particularly lucrative business for all the residents was harvesting.

Author Elizabeth Frame wrote about Chezzetcook in 1864:

Further up the harbor are groups of people busy digging clams. They are mostly lads and females. They turn up the soft mud with shovels then pick the clams into baskets and carry them to the shore, wading through the soft ooze a distance of several rods. (1 rod = about 5 metres) Further up are two women ditching—throwing the sods from their spades into a cart, which was drawn by a pair of oxen yoked by the horns.

The women of the community, she wrote, still maintained their traditional Acadian dress, "This head dress, kirtle and skirt, with buskins made of untanned hide, is, doubtless, very like that worn when DeMonts left France, nearly three centuries ago."

Ruins of Cole Harbour Bridge. *Photographed by Clara Dennis, probably about 1920.*

Today, the fishery has declined. Residents still harvest clams, but on a smaller scale. Some descendants of the Acadians who came here long ago remain in the area, and a small museum in West Chezzetcook interprets the life of the historic Acadian village for summer visitors.

Back at Cole Harbour, beginning in about 1830, "Squire" Jean George Bissett ran a ferry for a while between his property on the western side of the harbour and West Lawrencetown on the eastern side. In an attempt in the 1840s to reclaim some of the Cole Harbour marsh and create more productive farmland, work started on a dyke across the mouth of the harbour. The people of West Lawrencetown had hoped that this would incorporate a bridge over the harbour entrance to replace the ferry that had shortened their journey to Halifax, but they were disappointed as the dyking project was a failure. Eventually a new company was formed, and work on a dyke began in 1877. The marshy land was drained by a sluice gate, resembling the aboiteau system constructed by the Acadians, to let fresh water out from the enclosed land and prevent salt water from entering. A road ran along the dyke and a wooden bridge now allowed horse-drawn vehicles, and later cars, to cross the aboiteau.

Farming on the dykeland continued for some time, but the original company folded and Peter Kuhn, who lived at Upper Lawrencetown, bought the land in 1891. He attempted to keep the aboiteau repaired and to run a farm where he cut hay. It seems that the land was often poorly drained, wind and water frequently damaged the dyke, and maintaining it after winter storms was backbreaking work, as described by Peter Kuhn's granddaughter Margaret Kuhn Campbell:

The men of the household, which means father and two sons, even when the boys were of very tender age, would have to drive in the heavy farm wagon eight slow miles by the West Lawrencetown Road to the aboiteau, work all day according to the tide-governed opportunity, and return at night, often arriving late in the evening, only to leave early next morning for another hard day.

Despite the difficulties of maintenance, the dyke system lasted until 1917. At that time, some people objected to the sluice gate's interference with the flow of water and the passage of fish. One night the aboiteau was mysteriously destroyed. Some people maintained it was "blown up," and it was not rebuilt.

In about 1915, work began on the causeway to carry a railway line across the harbour. This was a major change to its configuration. Other changes came once the entrance was no longer controlled by the aboiteau. The alteration in the water flow caused sand dunes to build up, and a new channel was cut through the beach on the eastern side. The sand dunes now form the popular Rainbow Haven Beach.

To avoid encroachment from the expansion of Dartmouth and the loss of land to developers, residents banded together to have much of the shore area around the harbour protected. The Cole Harbour–Lawrencetown and Rainbow Haven Beach Provincial Parks now provide habitat for wildlife and recreational areas for city dwellers. Lawrencetown Beach has become a popular venue for surfers. The abandoned railway track across the harbour has become part of the Salt Marsh Trail, and the Cole Harbour Heritage Farm Museum recreates the days when the residents of Cole Harbour farmed their land and raised their animals, preserving this area's interesting history,

Afterword

Nova Scotia's stunning coastal scenery, and its compelling history, bring many visitors to this province, but those of us who live here often pass the scenery by in our hurry to reach our destinations, thinking that maybe some other day we might take the time to savour the riches on our doorstep. It is a mistake we are all guilty of, and it means we may miss a lot.

Following the old shore roads along Nova Scotia's coast brings plenty of rewards, though the journey may take longer. The route wanders round bays and headlands, past beaches and rocky cliffs. It leads to harbours where fishing gear lies on the wharves, and various types of fishing boats, from trawlers to Cape Islanders, are moored alongside. Lucky visitors may see their catches being unloaded or may partake of the bounty in nearby restaurants. Many communities have local museums where their history is narrated or recreated. The roads lead back to busy Halifax Harbour, home to naval and commercial shipping, cruise ships, ferries, and sailboats.

Not only are the bays and harbours of Nova Scotia extraordinarily beautiful, but as we have seen, many of them also have interesting tales to tell. In many places, the Mi'kmaq gathered each summer to set up their wigwams where they met and welcomed the first European fishing crews. In some, rival French entrepreneurs squabbled over their concessions. In other places the British and French garrisoned troops, or fought over control of the colony, while elsewhere settlers established fish-processing plants, sawmills, and shipyards. Many of these stories date from times when people were much more closely linked to the sea for their living than we are today.

There are many little harbours with interesting stories that I have been unable to include in the space of this book. In a province as rich with history as Nova Scotia, such omissions are inevitable, as communities may have very similar stories.

In order to avoid duplication, I have had to be selective. Please forgive me if I have left out your favourite harbour.

Only a few of the places I have written about are formally recognized as historic sites. Many of them are simply quiet reminders of people who lived and worked and helped to build this province, but they are all an important part of our history. So if you drive along our shores, take time to think about the people who came to these harbours long ago, the communities they created, and the events they witnessed.

Acknowledgements

Thanks, as always, are due to Garry Shutlak and the ever-helpful staff at the Nova Scotia Archives for their assistance in finding material; to Jocelyn Gillis of the Antigonish Heritage Museum; and to the curators and guides of many other museums where local history is preserved. My appreciation and admiration go to all the local historians whose books, pamphlets, brochures, and web pages record the stories of their communities. I am grateful to Mary Barker for snippets of her family history, to Deborah Trask for her expert knowledge of Mahone Bay, to Sara Beanlands who introduced me to the Thibodeau farm, and to Heather Laskey who invited me to Big Harbour. Thanks, too, to my family and friends for their support and their company on many of my journeys. My thanks are also due to Elizabeth Eve for her valuable suggestions as this book was taking shape, and to Trevor Sanipass for reviewing references in the text to Mi'kmaw place names and events. And my gratitude, once again, to Whitney Moran, Angela Mombourquette, and the rest of the team at Nimbus for their constant support over the years.

JD

BIBLIOGRAPHY

Most biographical material comes from the Dictionary of Canadian Biography, published by the University of Toronto Press from 1966 onwards, and available online. Another valuable source of information is the series of county maps published by Ambrose Church between 1865 and 1887.

PRINCIPAL BOOKS CONSULTED

Campbell, Margaret Kuhn. *Tale of Two Dykes: The Story of Cole Harbour.* Hantsport: Lancelot Press, 1979.

Chambers, Sheila, Joan Dawson, and Edith Wolter. *Historic LaHave River Valley.* Halifax: Nimbus Publishing, 2004.

Champlain, Samuel de. *Les Voyages du Sieur de Champlain.* Paris: Berjon, 1613. (Facsimile ed. Readex Microprint, 1966).

Chiasson, Père Anselme. *Chéticamp: Histoire et Traditions Acadiennes.* Moncton: Éditions des Aboiteaux, 1972.

Choyce, Lesley. *Nova Scotia, a Traveller's Companion: Over 300 years of Travel Writing.* Lawrencetown: Pottersfield Press, 2005.

Clark, Andrew Hill. *Acadia; The Geography of Early Nova Scotia to 1760.* Madison: University of Wisconsin Press, 1968.

Crowell, Edwin. *A History of Barrington Township and Vicinity, Shelburne County, Nova Scotia, 1604–1870.* Yarmouth: n.p., 1923.

Dawson, Joan. *Nova Scotia's Historic Rivers: The Waterways that Shaped the Province.* Halifax: Nimbus Publishing, 2012.

———. *A History of Nova Scotia in 50 Objects.* Halifax: Nimbus Publishing, 2015.

———. *The Mapmaker's Eye; Nova Scotia through Early Maps*. Halifax: Nimbus Publishing and The Nova Scotia Museum, 1988.

DesBrisay, Mather Byles. *History of the County of Lunenburg*. 2nd ed. Toronto: William Briggs, 1895.

Denys, Nicolas. *Description and Natural History of the Coasts of America (Acadia)*. Trans. and ed. William F. Ganong. Toronto: The Champlain Society, 1908.

Edwards, Tony. *Historic Bedford*. Halifax: Nimbus Publishing, 2007.

Fingard, Judith, Janet Guildford, and David Sutherland. *Halifax: The first 250 Years*. Halifax: Formac Publishing, 1999.

Fischer, David Hackett. *Champlain's Dream: The Visionary Explorer Who Made a New World In Canada*. Toronto: Vintage Canada, 2009.

Grant, John N. *Historic Guysborough*. Halifax: Nimbus Publishing, 2004.

Gwyn, Julian. "Shaped by the Sea but Impoverished by the Soil: Chester Township to 1830," in *The Nova Scotia Planters in the Atlantic World 1759–1830*, edited by Stephen T. Henderson & Wendy G. Robicheau. Fredericton: Acadiensis Press, 2012.

Johnson, A. J. B. "Avant les Loyalistes: Les Acadiens dans la Région de Sydney, 1749 à 1754" in *Les Cahiers* Vol. 19 no. 3, edited by La Société Historique Acadienne, 1988.

———. "The Fishermen of Eighteenth-Century Cape Breton: Numbers and Origins." *Nova Scotia Historical Review*, Vol. 9, No. 1, 1989.

Lescarbot, Marc. *Nova Francia, 1606*, trans. P. Erondelle, 1609. ed. E. D. Ross and E. Power. Harper Bros.: New York and London, 1928.

Loomer, L.S. *Windsor, Nova Scotia: A Journey into History*. Windsor, NS: West Hants Historical Society, 1996.

MacKay, Donald. *Scotland Farewell: The People of the Hector*. Toronto: McGraw Ryerson Limited, 1980.

McLennan, J. S. *Louisbourg: from its Foundation to its Fall 1713–1758*. Halifax: The Book Room Limited, 1979, reprinted 2000.

Marshall, Dianne. *Georges Island; The Keep of Halifax Harbour*. Halifax: Nimbus Publishing, 2003.

Mitcham, Allison. *Islands of Nova Scotia: Outpost Portraits*. Halifax: Nimbus Publishing, 2015.

Morse, William Inglis, ed. *Acadiensia Nova*. London: Quaritch, 1935.

Parker, Mike. *Historic Digby*. Halifax: Nimbus Publishing, 2000.

Perry, Hattie A. *A Bridge Over Time*. Barrington, NS: Spindrift Publishing, 2003.

Pothier, Don R. *History of Tusket Nova Scotia*. Tusket, NS: Argyle Municipality Historical and Genealogical Society, 2010.

Raddall, Thomas H. *Halifax, Warden of the North*. Halifax: Nimbus Publishing, 1993.

Ross, Sally, and Alphonse Deveau. *The Acadians of Nova Scotia Past and Present*. Halifax: Nimbus Publishing, 1992.

Sable, Trudy, and Bernie Francis. *The Language of this Land, Mi'kma'ki*. Sydney: Cape Breton University Press, 2012.

Service Nova Scotia and Municipal Relations and Nova Scotia Geomatics Centre. *The Nova Scotia Atlas* 5th ed. Halifax: Formac Publishing and the Province of Nova Scotia, 2001.

Shea, Iris, and Heather Watts. *Deadman's: Melville Island and its Burial Ground*. Glen Margaret, NS: Glen Margaret Publishing, 2005.

Sherwood, Roland H. *Pictou's Past*. Halifax: Lancelot Press, 1988.

Tennyson, Brian, and Wilma Stewart-White. *Historic Mahone Bay*. Halifax: Nimbus Publishing, 2006.

Timmins, Marion. *Wilderness Home: The Loyalist Founding of Country Harbour*. Glen Margaret, NS: Glen Margaret Publishing, 2010.

Watts, Heather, and Michèle Raymond. *Halifax's Northwest Arm: An Illustrated History*. Halifax: Formac Publishing, 2003.

Webster, John Clarence. *Acadia at the End of the Seventeenth Century; Letters, Journals and Memoirs of Joseph Robineau de Villebon and Other Contemporary Documents*. Sackville: New Brunswick Museum, 1934.

ONLINE SOURCES

Much information has been derived from the websites of communities and museums, and from digitized books on local history, often supplemented by articles from Wikipedia. Only the most important have been cited.

Acadian Census Records. acadian-home.org/census-acadia.html.

Brown, George Stayley. *Yarmouth, Nova Scotia: A Sequel to Campbell's History.* bit.ly/2RlLeVI.

Bull, Mary Kate. *Sandy Cove: The History of a Nova Scotia Village.* 3rd ed., 2013 issuu.com/sandycove/docs/sandy_cove_book.

Cole Harbour Heritage Farm. "Crossing Cole Harbour: From Ferry to Dyke then Rail to Trail." bit.ly/2xdhV0J.

Comeau, Delbé L. "Ship-building–Meteghan." claretownship.ca/?page_id=6672.

———. "Ship-building–Meteghan River (La Butte)." claretownship.ca/?page_id=6653.

Crowell, Doug. "John Smith, the man who owned the Money-Pit." oakislandcompendium.ca/blockhouse-blog/john-smith-the-man-who-owned-the-money-pit.

Digby, Nova Scotia. "Town History." digby.ca/town-history.html.

East Hants. "Local History: Maitland." easthants.com/history.htm.

Eskasoni. "History of Eskasoni." eskasoni.ca/History/.

Gough, Joseph. "History of Commercial Fisheries." *The Canadian Encyclopedia.* thecanadianencyclopedia.ca/en/article/history-of-commercial-fisheries.

Grant, John. "The Development of Sherbrooke Village to 1880." sherbrookevillage.novascotia.ca/sites/default/files/inline/documents/history_of_sherbrooke_village.pdf.

LaHave Islands Marine Museum. "Island Industry: Fishing and Fish Plants." lahaveislandsmarinemuseum.ca/industry.html.

Mcinnis, Peter S., Heather MacDonald, and Birgitta Wallace. "Canso." *The Canadian Encyclopedia.* thecanadianencyclopedia.ca/en/article/canso.

Musée des Acadiens des Pubnicos et Centre de recherche. "Brief History of Pubnico." museeacadien.ca/english/history/brief.htm.

Pellerin, Brad. "The Acadians of Tor Bay, Guysborough County; The Chezzetcook Connection." guyscogene.net/places/acadians.html.

Pinaud, Mary. "History of Baddeck." baddeck.com/history.

Region of Queens County Municipality. "Coffin Island." regionofqueens.com/visit/experience/attractions/lighthouses/coffin-island.

St. Peters. "Village History." visitstpeters.com/village-history/.

Seccombe, John. "Journal of Rev. John Seccombe." Nova Scotia Archives. novascotia.ca/archives/townships/archivesX.asp?ID=8&Page=201104216&Language.

Société des Acadiens de la Région de Tor Bay. "Forgotten Acadians." socacadien.org/forgotten-acadians/.

Town of Shelburne, Nova Scotia. "Shelburne's History." town.shelburne.ns.ca/shelburnes-history.html.

The Village of Havre Boucher Nova Scotia Canada. "History." havreboucher.com/index.php/community/history.

Village of Pugwash. "History." pugwashvillage.com/index.php/living-in-pugwash/history.

Image Credits

Dawson, Joan: 96, 97, 104
Library of Congress: 23
Lunenburg County Historical Society: 56, 81
Nova Scotia Archives: 9, 21, 24, 31, 34, 41, 44, 52, 61, 67, 73, 78, 85, 88, 92, 101, 109, 110, 116, 122, 127, 129, 137, 139, 143, 148, 155, 161, 169, 170, 174

Also by Joan Dawson

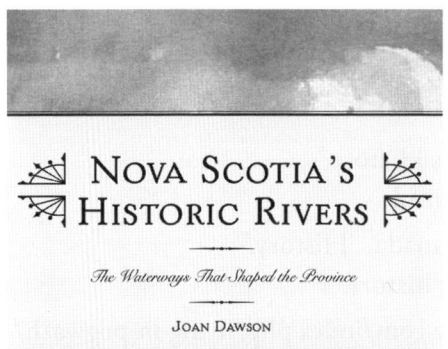

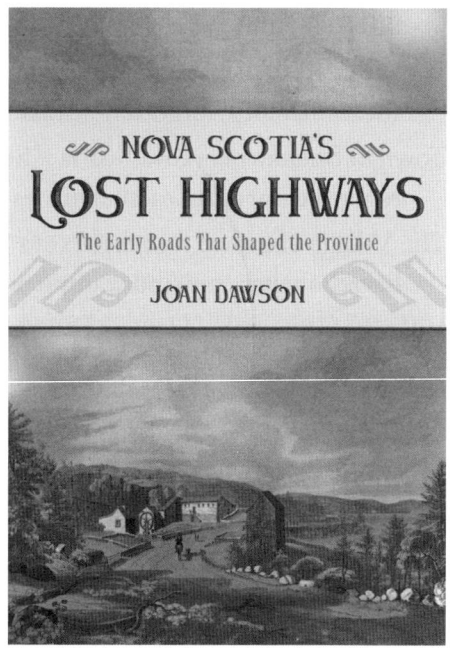

ISBN: 978-1-55109-932-3

ISBN: 978-1-55109-732-9

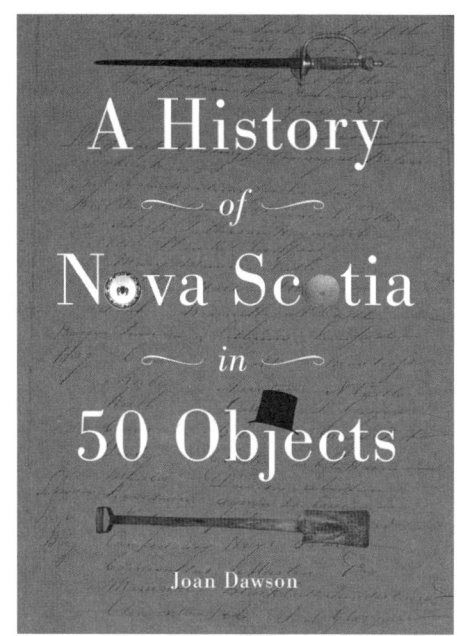

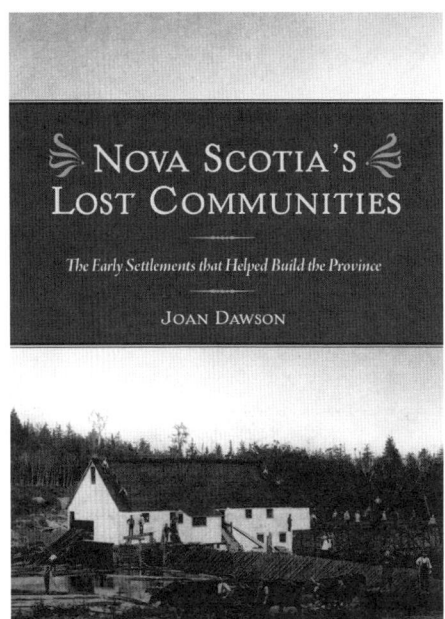

ISBN: 978-1-77108-603-5

ISBN: 978-1-77108-295-2

Available at fine bookstores and online at nimbus.ca